Cornwall's Great Gardens

To Charles and Howard..........may your love of gardens grow with your years. T.R.

To my Mother and Father who are greatly missed. D.H.

Cornwall's Great Gardens

Foreword by **H.R.H. The Prince of Wales**

Photography by **Derek Harris**   *Text by* **Tony Russell**

First Published in 1998
Reprinted in 2003
by
The WoodLand & Garden Publishing Company
Holmleigh Farm, Huntsgate, Gedney Broadgate, Spalding, Lincs, PE12 0DJ

Photography Copyright Derek Harris
Text Copyright Tony Russell

ISBN   1 899803 05 X

Designed by Derek Harris and Associates Limited.
Origination and Film Sets by Goodfellow & Egan Limited, Peterborough.
Printed and Bound in Great Britain by Butler and Tanner Limited, Frome.

Pictures used in this book and other photographic work by Derek Harris is available from
The WoodLand & Garden Publishing Company
Holmleigh Farm, Huntsgate, Gedney Broadgate, Spalding, Lincs, PE12 0DJ
Telephone: 01406 366503   Fax: 01406 366502
Email: derekharris.associates@virgin.net

Introduction Pictures
Cover Lanhydrock National Trust Garden
Page 1 Orchids at Chyverton
Page 4 Treve Holman Memorial Bridge at Chyverton
Page 8 Tree Ferns at Trebah
Pages 10/11 Cypress trees and lavender at Tresco Abbey Gardens

CONTENTS

Foreword 9

Introduction 12-13

Information on Cornish Gardens 14

The Gardens 15

Cotehele 16-27

Antony 28-37

Lanhydrock 38-51

Heligan 52-63

Caerhays 64-73

Trewithen 74-83

CONTENTS

Chyverton — 84-95

Trelissick — 96-107

Glendurgan — 108-117

Trebah — 118-131

Trengwainton — 132-141

Tresco Abbey — 142-155

Photographic Notes — 156

Acknowledgements — 157

Index — 158-160

I am always intrigued, on my travels through Britain, to see just how few of our trees, shrubs and other plants are truly native to this country. There are, for instance, thought to be only thirty four different types of British native tree. The rest, which run into thousands, have all been introduced at some time or another from every corner of the temperate world. It is in some ways no surprise that so many of the plants we may see daily in our local parks and gardens have been introduced, for Britain has one of the best climates for plant growing in the world. We may not like cool, wet summers, but plants definitely do!

We owe a tremendous debt to those great plant collectors who, over the last hundred and fifty years, risked life and limb to introduce to Britain the cream of the world's flora. Indeed, there can be few gardens in Britain today which do not contain plants introduced by David Douglas, George Forrest, Frank Kingdon-Ward and E. H. Wilson, to name just four. My own gardens at Highgrove are a case in point.

Long before the days of commercial horticulture, many of these early plant introductions found their way into country estates and were the catalyst for the creation of some of our greatest gardens. It became apparent early on that certain areas of Britain provided more favourable growing conditions than others – especially those areas influenced by the Gulf Stream and boasting good sandy loam soil, slightly on the acid side. Cornwall in particular was ideal, and it was not long before a steady stream of rhododendrons, azaleas, camellias and magnolias found their way across the River Tamar into estates such as Caerhays Castle, Lanhydrock, Tresco and Trewithen. These estates, and several others, now contain some of the greatest gardens, not just in Cornwall, but in Britain and possibly the world at large. Over the years it has been my privilege to visit many of them.

This marvellous book brings together the greatest of these Cornish gardens, and through its sensitive text and stunning photography captures their very essence. I believe it will encourage those of us who know them well to re-visit. For those who are unfamiliar with them I hope it will provide the impetus to begin a wonderful journey of discovery through the great gardens of Cornwall.

Introduction

Shortly after Derek Harris and I discussed the idea of creating a book on the great gardens of Cornwall, I happened to visit a garden in south east England that had suffered terribly during the great storm of 1987. I was there to return a young *Hakea lissosperma*, a curious, pine-like tree with sharply pointed grey-green leaves. Until the storm, this particular garden had boasted the largest specimen in the country, an original introduction from south eastern Australia in 1929. My plant had been grown at Westonbirt Arboretum from a cutting, taken from the original tree as it lay on the ground in those chaotic days following the 17th October 1987. Returning the young plant would ensure at least part of the original continued to grow, in this garden, in much the same way as it had done during the previous sixty years.

On my arrival, I was met by the Head Gardener, who proceeded to take me on a tour of the grounds. Half way round we passed the original *Hakea lissosperma*, carefully propped up and covered with hessian sacking to protect its blistering trunk from sun scorch. "It may live", he said, with some considerable doubt in his voice. Then, with a deep sigh, he gazed around and quietly said, "this used to be a truly great garden".

During my drive home I thought about his words and the deep sense of sadness that had accompanied them. What was it that had made this garden great, and now, what was it that had changed all that, at least in the eyes of this particular head gardener? Was it the loss of some seventy per cent of its mature trees, or was that in itself too simple an explanation? What is it that makes any garden great, what is this thing we call greatness? Indeed, what did Derek and I have in mind as we considered bringing just a few, of the many Cornish gardens together under the banner, 'Cornwall's Great Gardens'. One thing I was sure of, 'great' didn't necessarily mean large, old or famous, it was something more personal than that.

I started to think about all of the gardens I had spent time in and what each one had meant to me. Was there something in common between those that I had enjoyed, thought of as special and had wanted to return to? My earliest recollection of a garden that fell into this category was my grandfather's. It certainly wasn't famous and probably, not that old. To a five-year old child gazing longingly at ripe, juicy fruit, hanging from the top most boughs of the peach tree, it did seem quite large, but that wasn't what made it great. It had a pond, the surface of which, in springtime, was almost purple as it reflected the many bluebells around its edge. I remember there were several other fruit trees, mainly apples and a passion flower growing vigorously over a rustic trellis. Flowers, there were plenty, especially dahlias, great pom-poms of colour, which in late summer were cut and brought into the parlour. I can still smell their fragrance, which seemed to permeate through every room of my grandparents' small cottage. A white timber framed greenhouse near the bottom of the garden was filled with a vast array of cacti and other succulents, beyond which stood an old shed, made from the remains of an Anderson shelter, which had been at the furthest point of the garden. I loved that garden and just remembering it brings back that great rush of excitement and expectancy I used to experience on hearing the back door click behind me. Seconds later I would be rushing down the brick and cinder path to explore, once again, every inch of paradise. It was a truly great garden and the happiness and enjoyment it gave me lives on, even though, in reality it disappeared years ago. The last time I looked, it was even difficult to work out where the boundary fence had stood, most of the area having been given over to housing and tarmac some 20 years ago.

I continued to ponder over what made a great garden, until the time came for Derek and I to select the gardens to be included in this book and then it all seemed to become clear. Neither of us could consider including a garden which meant we had to struggle to find the inspiration necessary, to create a portrait, which would in turn inspire others. A great garden must inspire, it must create an excitement and expectancy on entering and, on leaving, instil a feeling that the day has been special and will live on in memory months, even years after the visit.

So, in a way, the gardens featured selected themselves. This meant that some quite famous gardens, which we had from the beginning assumed would be in this book, were excluded and others, perhaps less well known, were plucked from relative obscurity. There are over sixty gardens, regularly open to the public in Cornwall, but to do justice to those included in this book, we limited our selection to just twelve. Given more space, I can think of several others which would have been included, perhaps their turn will come.

For Derek and I, the twelve gardens selected are truly great. They are unique, magical, inspirational and we feel a great affinity for them all. The words and photographs you find within this book are not really ours, they belong to the gardens; we wrote all the words and took all the photographs but they were offered to us willingly by the spirit of each and every garden. They were simply lying there, waiting to be found and appreciated. Having done that, we have created something, which we hope, will provide inspiration enough to set others off, on their own unique voyage of discovery through some of the greatest gardens in the world.

Tony Russell
January 1998

13

THE NATIONAL TRUST IN CORNWALL

The National Trust maintains seven major gardens in Cornwall on behalf of the nation. From Antony in the east to Trengwainton in the west, each garden reflects its own unique history and the families who created them.

Every year, over half a million visitors come to enjoy this rich variety, many returning time and again to enjoy the changing seasons.

Some of the gardens are home to National Plant Collections; all have plant sales areas, stocked with plants grown in Cornwall.

Each garden aspires to high and appropriate horticultural standards provided by skilled and devoted gardeners. New talent is encouraged by the Trust's own training scheme. Volunteers give invaluable help – and more are always welcome.

We hope you will enjoy the garden's described in this welcome volume. Further information about opening times and visitor facilities, including some access during the winter, is available from the property or from the Cornwall Regional Office, Lanhydrock, Bodmin PL30 4DE. Telephone: 01208 74281.

Peter Mansfield
Director of Cornwall

THE CORNWALL TOURIST BOARD

Each year the Cornwall Tourist Board in conjunction with the Cornwall Gardens Society, promotes the Cornwall Festival of Spring Gardens, which takes place from early March to the end of May, with approximately 70 gardens open to the public.

The Country Spring Flower Show is held over 3 days in mid-April. For further details and a programme of gardens open for the Festival, and indeed the rest of the year, please contact the Cornwall Tourist Board, Lander Building, Daniell Road Centre, Truro, Cornwall, TR1 2DA. Telephone: 01872 274057.

THE CORNWALL GARDEN SOCIETY

Cornwall Garden Society has diversified over the years and now takes in a wide spectrum of interests under their 'garden' umbrella.

With a membership of over 1500 its objective is "To Seek and Foster a Love and Knowledge of Gardening & Plants". Their County Spring Flower Show remains a major point of focus; its centenary year, 1997, drew some 23,000 visitors.

Lectures form another major aspect for the Society and they boast a series of some 26 lectures from September to April using nine venues in four different areas of this 100 mile long County, whilst their widely respected Annual Journal 'The Cornish Garden' published in March, is a record of horticultural happenings and developments in Cornish gardens and gardening.

Visits to gardens both within and outside the County forms yet another wing of activity, as do their educational "Workshops" and practical demonstrations.

Membership seems good value for money, with concessions available for some categories.

Membership and full details of the annual programme is available from the Cornwall Garden Society, Membership Secretary, Poltisko, Silver Hill, Perranwell Station, Truro, Cornwall, TR3 7LP. Telephone/Fax: 01872 86330.

The Gardens

Cotehele
The National Trust
St. Dominick
Saltash
PL12 6TA
Tel: 01579 351 346

Antony
The National Trust
Torpoint

PL11 2QA
Tel: 01752 812 191

Lanhydrock
The National Trust
Bodmin

PL30 5AD
Tel: 01208 73320

The Lost Gardens of Heligan
Mr. Tim Smit
Nr. Mevagissey
St. Austell
PL26 6EN
Tel: 01726 844 157

Caerhays Castle
F.J. Williams Esq. CBE
Gorran
St. Austell
PL26 6LY
Tel: 01872 501 144

Trewithen
A.M.J. Galsworthy Esq.
Grampound Road
Nr. Truro
TR2 4DD
Tel: 01726 883 647

Chyverton
N.T. Holman Esq.
Zelah
Nr. Truro
TR4 9HD
Tel: 01872 540 324

Trelissick
The National Trust
Feock
Nr. Truro
TR3 6QL
Tel: 01872 862 090

Glendurgan
The National Trust
Mawnan Smith
Nr. Falmouth
TR11 5JZ
Tel: 01326 250 906

Trebah
Trebah Garden Trust
Mawnan Smith
Nr. Falmouth
TR11 5JZ
Tel: 01326 250 448

Trengwainton
The National Trust
Penzance

TR20 8SA
Tel: 01736 363 021

Tresco Abbey
R.A. Dorrien-Smith Esq.
Tresco
Isles of Scilly
TR24 0QQ
Tel: 01720 422 849

More details on the gardens with opening dates, times and a useful map is available and shown
in the annual **"Gardens of Cornwall Open Guide"** available from

The Cornwall Tourist Board or The Cornwall Garden Society

Lander Building
Daniell Road Centre
Truro, Cornwall, TR1 2DA
Telephone 01872 274057

Poltisko, Silver Hill,
Perranwell Station
Truro, Cornwall, TR3 7LP
Telephone/Fax 01872 86330

Information and opening times of National Trust gardens is available from the properties or the
Cornwall Regional Office, Lanhydrock, Bodmin, PL30 4DE. Telephone 01208 74281

Cotehele

Cotehele

As I head my car westwards and leave the final M5 junction behind, I experience a familiar feeling stirring inside me, a wonderful mixture of excitement and expectancy.

Memories flood back of the last walk home from school at the end of the summer term. Ahead lay endless sunny days of freedom. What to do first, play in the park, the woods, meet with friends not seen since Easter?

Thirty years on, as I travel the A30 towards Launceston, my mind rushes ahead. Where to go first … which old friend shall I seek out this very day? The excitement, the expectancy, just the same as on that last day of term, only now, the friends are quite different. I am on my way to Cornwall and more exactly, once more to embark on the Cornish garden trail.

My mind made up, I head for Tavistock and that first friend, a truly Cornish garden, just across the Tamar … Cotehele.

I have visited Cotehele at just about every time of the year except winter, but for me it is at its best on a spring day with the sun shining brightly. High grassy banks topped with hawthorn, in bud but not yet in flower, line the roadside, bedecked in primroses and wild daffodils. The route to the garden follows great swathes of *Narcissi* up the drive and on into the main car park, which is sheltered by lichen and ivy covered mature oaks and sycamores. From here a path leads beneath an old flat topped Monterey Pine, *Pinus radiata*, through a little copse and out onto open lawns. It is here that one gets a first view of the low, grey granite and buff stone mediaeval house and the 18th century Prospect Tower on the hill beyond.

Owned since 1947 by the National Trust, Cotehele was until that time the property of the Edgcumbe family, who are perhaps better known for Mount Edgcumbe, their estate near Plymouth. The Edgcumbes settled at Cotehele in the 14th century. It wasn't however until the 19th century, that the gardens were laid out to their present design.

There are a multitude of delightful buildings in and around the estate, but none more so than the magnificent 15th century tithe barn with its incredible undulating slate roof which seems to mimic the rolling vistas of the surrounding countryside. It now contains the restaurant. Adjacent to the barn and standing on the edge of the old bowling green are three large sycamores, beneath which drifts of *Narcissi* and *Anemones* spread out from their base. The largest sycamore is some 150 years old and has wire braces to hold its great limbs together and prevent breakage during the frequent winter squalls which rush up the Tamar from the coast.

The verdant, close shaved bowling green is bordered by an interesting array of trees and shrubs including a Paperbark Maple, *Acer griseum* and a twenty feet tall, glossy willow-leaved, Podocarpus, *Podocarpus salignus*, which is in fact a conifer originating from Chile. For me though, one of the loveliest features of this corner of Cotehele is the wonderful old dry stone wall at the far end of the green. It is simply encrusted with lichen, moss and fern, and leans back in gentle repose like some whiskered old gentleman. There are views over the wall to the parkland beyond the garden, and then, on turning to re-trace one's steps, quite unexpectedly, the finest view of the house and its many outbuildings is revealed. It looks like a miniature walled town, each roof lying haphazardly on top of another, clambering and clustering upwards towards the main Western Tower. Despite the battlements, the house feels warm and inviting. Bright spring sunshine highlights the brown and grey south facing walls, against which brilliant red claw-like flowers of the Lobster Claw, *Clianthus puniceus* confirm this is indeed one of the warmest spots in the garden. A Climbing Hydrangea, *Hydrangea petiolaris* grows alongside and another covers the northern end of the great barn.

It is from here that the first breathtaking view of the gardens opens out, producing a stunning display of colour. In the foreground is the splendid formality of the terrace, giving way to the seemingly haphazard plantings of the Valley Garden, which tumbles away eastwards, down a wooded combe towards the Tamar. Bubbling up from this combe are literally thousands of red, pink and white blooms from a multitude of magnolias and rhododendrons. Any last lingering doubts about the Cornish-ness and indeed greatness of this garden are dispelled at this point.

Cotehele is a diverse collection of gardens, some extremely intimate, some wild and untamed, remarkably coming together to form a successful cohesive patchwork of landscapes. There are walled gardens, ancient orchards, herbaceous borders, terraces, valley gardens, ponds, streams and formal courtyards. It is to the latter I turn first.

Ducking beneath a stone archway, surrounded by *Ceanothus* and roses and surmounted by a weathered coat of arms, I enter the Hall Court. Here the paths are cobbled with up-ended pebbles and the high walls punctured with metal studded oak doors and leaded mullioned

Previous pages 5. Daffodil Meadow at Cotehele

windows, which peer formidably at those who venture into the court. A knarled old *Wisteria*, hung gracefully with a profusion of mauve flowers does its best to soften the atmosphere, but I, like many before me, quicken my step and move swiftly beneath a further archway into the even smaller Retainer's Court beyond, leaving behind just the echoing clatter of shoe leather on pebble.

In the Retainer's Court, *Camellias* grow straight out of the shiny grey cobbled floor, their sombre green leaves seeming to intensify the shadows. Almost apologetically, fallen soft white flowers from *Camellia* 'Cornish Snow' lay gently upon the hard grey irregular surface. I emerge into the warm sunshine and stand on the edge of a delightful sloping grassy meadow. It is covered with some twenty-seven varieties of *Narcissi*, displaying every daffodil colour imaginable from white to golden yellow. As a slight Cornish breeze runs through the meadow their heads rhythmically nod together as if coming to some unanimous agreement. Depending on the month, this meadow is covered with snowdrops, crocuses, wood anemones, celandines, bluebells, *Cyclamen* and *Colchicum*. In the north-east corner stands a magnificent specimen of the Strawberry Tree, *Arbutus x andrachnoides*, its rich cinnamon-red trunk and branches visible from every part of the meadow. In the centre of the meadow is one of the largest ornamental trees at Cotehele, a Tulip Tree, *Liriodendron tulipifera*. Its lime-yellow flowers not appearing until the last bluebell has faded.

One of my favourite walks at Cotehele at any time of year but particularly in spring, is along the upper pathway which borders the top of the daffodil meadow. From here there are views back across the meadow to the house and beyond to the rolling hills of Devon. The range of plants along this path is truly inspiring. There are Mediterranean Cork Oaks, *Quercus suber* with deeply fissured bark, the Chilean Lantern Bush, *Crinodendron hookerianum* and from New Zealand, *Griselinia littoralis* with its lovely leathery leaves and short green flower spikes. Just a stride away is another Southern Hemisphere plant *Drimys lanceolata* from Tasmania, but the crowning glory for me has to be *Acacia pravissima*, the Oven's Wattle, from Australia. It is positively frothing with deliciously fragrant, clear yellow flowers which contrast delightfully against its curiously shaped olive-green leaves (known as phyllodes), looking just as if they have been cut off half way up with a pair of scissors.

A gate close by leads northwards out of the garden towards a line of weather beaten old pine trees which stride purposefully across the hillside in the direction of the Prospect Tower some 500 yards away. Pleasingly, the door to the tower remains unlocked, encouraging those with a head for heights to climb the replacement wooden steps to the view point. It is well worth the climb; from the top the prospect of the Cornish-Devon border is quite superb. Below lies the Tamar Valley, the tidal river crossed by a twelve arched railway viaduct seemingly just a stone's throw away. Beyond the river the village of Calstock is backed by fresh green Devon hills which roll away eastwards, giving way as the land rises, to the rock strewn slopes of Dartmoor in the distance. Up here the air is never still and the skylarks seem always to sing.

Back on ground level, entering the Upper Garden, one is immediately aware of the sound of running water. A small rivulet splashes out from the wall, flows beneath the path and on down the grassy slope into the lily pool. Alongside runs a hedge of Mexican Orange Blossom, *Choisya ternata*. When in bloom, in late spring, its heady fragrance fills the garden, flowering on until the expanding plants within the herbaceous borders are ready to perform. *Agapanthus*, *Fuchsias*, *Kniphofias*, day lilies and *Papavers* bring rich summer colours to beds which lay beneath the warm garden walls, where wooden seats facing the pool beckon those with a mind for contemplation.

Beyond close clipped yew hedges lies The Nursery and formal cutting garden. It is here that all the flowers for the house are grown, a mixture of bulbs, annuals and perennials, mostly of cottage garden type. Upright, Japanese Locust trees, *Gleditsia japonica* stand in each corner and peeping out over the tall yew hedge is a splendid Pride of India, *Koelreuteria paniculata*. This has to be one of my favourite trees for spring colour, the foliage on emerging from the bud is a wonderful apricot-pink colour.

No self-respecting Cornish garden is complete without a Chusan Palm, *Trachycarpus fortunei*. It adds that sense of exotica with its large, fan shaped, many fingered leaves and shaggy, coconut-like fibrous bark. Cotehele is no exception, it has several in the valley garden and one notable specimen in the nursery area, not far from a gigantic Golden Ash, *Fraxinus excelsior* 'Jaspidea'.

A little secret doorway cut into the yew hedging leads from The Nursery and Upper Garden into a garden with sloping raised beds and then into an old cider orchard. Now this is what an orchard should look like, full size fruit trees with knarled bark and twisted branches that meet in mid-air, creating a canopy of leaf and blossom, beneath which wild flowers run riot. At one end of the orchard, growing out of the herbage is a cluster of freshly painted white bee-hives. It is just about the most perfect setting imaginable. What a peaceful, tranquil place this is. It would be very easy to simply sit in the warm spring afternoon sunshine and catch up with one's thoughts, or even just watch the plants grow! There are some who visit Cotehele only to experience the Valley Garden, which is a shame, for they are experiencing only a part of this great garden. It is a garden with surprises around every corner and should be explored to the full. It naturally follows then, that my visit would be incomplete without a walk from the Eastern Terrace, down through the Valley Garden to the banks of the Tamar. So, like a child about to un-wrap a long promised gift, I make my way in that direction, passing through a delightful maple dell on the way. The dell is deliberately planted to provide stunning displays of leaf colour in autumn. There are Katsura Trees, *Cercidiphyllum japonicum*, Dawn Redwoods, *Metasequoia glybtostroboides* and of course Japanese Maples, *Acer palmatum*. Definitely a spot to return to in early October.

Arriving on the Eastern Terrace at the head of the Valley Garden, the view down the combe towards the Tamar is quite marvellous. No lime in the soil here, rhododendrons abound, Cornish Reds (or if you are on the other side of the river, Devon Pinks) intermingle with large, white, Tree Heathers, *Erica arborea* var. *alpina*, which droop low over pathways, casting their sweet vanilla-like fragrance in every direction. The Eastern Terrace was laid out on three levels after 1862. The two lower levels have rose borders underplanted with *Aubrieta* and silver-leaved Lamb's Ears, *Stachys byzantina*. There are formal plantings of variegated, Japanese Angelica trees *Aralia elata* 'Variegata' and young *soulangeana* magnolias alongside stone seating. The magnolias were planted to replace the old specimens lost during the storms of January 1990. Lead urns flank the stone steps that lead from the Eastern door of the house to the foot of the terrace, where one finds an arbour of Rose Acacia, *Robinia hispida*. From here, one catches a glimpse of pure white doves perched on the domed roof of a stone dovecote further down the valley, and spectacular views across to Nellson's Piece, a two acre arboretum planted up mainly in the last twenty five years with a number of rare and tender trees, including many magnolias, a handkerchief tree, *Davidia involucrata* and several Asian *Acers*.

From the arbour, the path follows a stone parapet which is being over-run in all directions by a tidal wave of large deep pink, goblet shaped magnolia blooms. Down a steep flight of steps and through a dark stone tunnel, it spills out between dense shrubs into the sheltered environment of the Valley Garden. Here, one finds further remnants of an earlier age, a mediaeval stewpond, filled with Golden Orfe, at one time used to feed the residents of the house and the handsome round dovecote, seen from the arbour above. From deep within its mossy stonework on this quiet spring evening, a gentle rhythmic cooing can be heard. The sound travels towards an enchanting thatched summer house close by. Overhung by tree rhododendrons of gigantic proportions, this rustic resting place looks down onto the stewpond and provides a perfect opportunity to linger and soak up the serenity of this secluded woodland garden.

From the pond a small rill trickles down the centre of the valley, its verdant banks covered with kingcups, candelabra *Primulas*, *Hostas*, Skunk Cabbage, *Lysichiton americanus* and *Polystichum setiferum*, the Soft shield fern. Later on in the year, enormous leaves of *Gunnera manicata* will provide a dense canopy, preventing the hottest sunshine from reaching the woodland floor. As one meanders down the valley, great forests of laurel provide effective screening and add to the seclusion.

This is a wonderful voyage of discovery for anyone even remotely interested in plants. Every few paces yet another botanical jewel reveals itself and then quietly slips back into the surrounding vegetation once you have passed by. Many were introduced by the 3rd Earl of Mount Edgcumbe more than 130 years ago. An enormous *Enkianthus cernuus* var. *rubens*, *Corylopsis willmottiae* with soft yellow, fragrant flowers dripping from every bough. *Pinus patula*, the Spread-Leaved Pine from Mexico, with the finest needles on any pine tree you will ever see. They are grey-green, up to ten inches long and hang gracefully in clusters. As one looks up through the foliage it appears almost smokey against the blue sky. A Himalayan birch, *Betula utilis* with its creamy white flaking bark and close by, so at home in this sheltered valley of such high humidity is a *Dicksonia antarctica*, the Soft tree fern from Australia and Tasmania.

Further down the combe the exotic vegetation reverts to native woodland. The path continues on down to the Tamar and Cotehele Quay, passing on its way a charming little chapel in the woods, built in 1490 by Sir Richard Edgcumbe as a thank-you offering for his escape from his enemies on this spot in 1483. The coolness of the white-washed walls and stone floor provides a welcome resting place for those making their way from the Quay to the gardens. There are walks from the Quay along the Tamar in both directions, but for me there is only one direction, and that is to re-trace my steps back up the valley to spend a bit longer with an old Cornish friend.

Opposite 6. View over the combe to Calstock village and the Tamar railway viaduct

7. Bluebells following the daffodils in The Meadow

8. Old sycamore by the tithe barn

9. Through rhododendrons to the east front of the house

10. View into the combe with the dovecote and stewpond

11. Thatched summer house with cherry blossom

12. Summer house with *Rhododendron* 'Cornish Red'

13. Medieval domed dovecote and stewpond

15. Clematis on wall by east front of house

Opposite 16. *Leptospermum scoparium* in the Upper Garden

14. Rambling roses on an outbuilding

17. View of sycamores and daffodils to the house

18. Hall Court

19. East front of the house with formal terrace below

20. Crimson *Rhododendron russellianum* to east front of house

21. Variegated Japanese Angelica trees on the terrace

22. Herbaceous border in the Upper Garden

23. Red floribunda roses in the formal terrace

Antony

Antony House and Woodland Garden

If Heligan is considered to be the 'lost garden' of Cornwall, then Antony must surely be the 'undiscovered garden'.

I, like thousands of others before me, had passed close to its boundary many times over the years as I made my way southwards to the historic gardens of Mount Edgcumbe, close to Plymouth Sound. It wasn't however until the spring of 1995 that, almost by chance, I turned off the A374 and found myself on a concrete drive, passing through lush green parkland, dotted with ancient oaks uniformly browsed by generations of sheep. Little did I know, that along this drive, lay one of the loveliest gardens in the whole of England.

I had spent the previous night in Plymouth and rose early to catch the first morning ferry from Devonport, across the Tamar to Torpoint. The crossing lasts only minutes but this narrow strip of sparkling blue water is enough to turn the clock back centuries.

Half way down the drive, the view of Plymouth across the estuary disappears and with it the last trace of the hustle and bustle of twentieth century life. A single column of lime trees, on either side of the drive, casts dappled shade upon thousands of celandines, those first smiling faces of spring and overhead the mew of a circling buzzard cuts through the clear, cool air. Then, through the trees, a first glimpse of Antony House, a handsome grey stone building, unpretentious and yet imaginative. Its curtilage defined by rose covered walls and a magnificent set of black iron gates, replicas of those that stand at the entrance to Carew Manor, near Beddington in Surrey.

Antony House was built by Sir William Pole-Carew in the early years of the eighteenth century, to replace a Tudor mansion close by, which had been home to the Carew family since 1432. The Carew-Poles still live at Antony (the priority to the name changed in the early part of this century) and today, Sir Richard Carew-Pole, takes great pride in maintaining and indeed developing a series of gardens laid out by his forebears. Many changes to the gardens have taken place over the years, possibly the most dramatic occurring in 1792, when the Rt. Hon. Reginald Pole-Carew, "a minister of the crown and a man of great taste", invited the most influential landscape gardener of the day, Humphrey Repton, to advise on the garden. Repton's advice, presented in one of his famous red books, (and still in the family's possession), was in part taken up. Some of the formal walled gardens immediately in front of the house were cleared, replaced by a more natural parkland landscape with long vistas and informal tree planting. This mixture of formality and informality is still evident today, to such an extent that Antony can justifiably be said to have two gardens. An arrangement of formal gardens close to the house, managed today by the National Trust and then beyond, a wild, woodland garden looked after by the Carew-Pole Garden Trust. It is this wonderful mixture of landscapes that makes Antony so special and for me on my first visit so unexpected and exciting.

Having parked my car, I first decided to explore the formal gardens, which mainly lay to the north and west of the house. A long gravel terrace runs the length of the northern aspect, at the eastern end of which stands a delightful red brick circular dovecote, one of the oldest features in the garden, it still has white doves in residence. Beyond can be seen avenues of weeping lime, *Tilia x euchlora* striding eastwards across rich green undulating parkland. From the terrace, a great lawn runs away northwards, interrupted only by an enormous Black Walnut, *Juglans nigra* and two sombre clumps of Holm Oak, *Quercus ilex*, planted in the 1760's. In the distance the River Lynher is just visible as a thin ribbon of light, glinting in the early spring sunshine, as it flows from the peaty uplands of Bodmin Moor to the tidal reaches of the Tamar. Great mounds of Ceanothus tumble down either side of tread worn steps, engulfing stone urns at the foot of the terrace. Close by and found only by following the faintest sound of trickling water, lies a small Japanese garden. Designed by the late Sir John Carew-Pole, it contains pebble paths, stone Buddha and a lily filled pond into which dips the delicate fern-like foliage of a Japanese Maple, *Acer palmatum* 'Dissectum'. From the Japanese garden and running the full length of the terrace is a border overflowing with roses and vigorous drifts of *Nepeta sintenisii* 'Six Hills Giant'. Although planted for summer colour, on this spring morning there are already signs of early purple-blue catmint flowers, giving just a hint of displays yet to come.

Where the terrace ends, at the north western corner of the house, there is more water, but this time used in a much less conventional way. A superb sculpture entitled 'Watercone', thrusts itself skywards, water spilling from the apex of the cone and flowing, like some viscous liquid, down its glistening flanks. Designed by young sculptor William Pye in 1995, its inspiration is just yards away. An enormous yew hedge, planted in 1780, runs westwards from the house and contains a magnificent piece of yew topiary in the form of a closely clipped cone more than thirty feet tall. Some two hundred years separates these two works of art

Previous pages 24. Antony House with stormy sky

and yet so comfortably they sit together in this garden of contrasts.

Moving away from the house I follow a path alongside the yew hedge, the far side of which is an avenue of free standing *Magnolia grandiflora* with glossy, deep green leaves, shimmering in the sun which is now beginning to warm my back. Beside the magnolias lies a flat level lawn which used to be the Antony tennis courts. It is said that Lady Carew-Pole, (grandmother to the present Sir Richard), longed for somewhere cool and shady to sit and enjoy the family contests which took place on this old court. So she asked the Head Gardener of the time to cut out an arch in the conical yew, just deep enough to take a small wooden bench. Cool and shady it certainly was but Lady Carew-Pole hadn't reckoned on every midge and mosquito in the garden wanting to share the spot with her, consequently it wasn't used that often. Nevertheless, it is still today a remarkable place to sit. Sunshine filters through the yew's dense evergreen foliage, creating illuminated patterns on the rich, blood red bark and pollen dust, from a disturbed branch, dances upwards through a succession of sunbeams. Gazing across the lawn from this little wooden bench it is very easy to drift back to some long forgotten Edwardian afternoon and hear the echoing thwack of tennis ball against racket, followed by an excited cry from some straw hatted young lady.

The lawn extends well beyond the boundary of the old tennis court and is dotted with mature, open-grown specimen trees including a Black Walnut, *Juglans nigra* and an Oriental Plane, *Platanus orientalis*. The finest tree by far is a quite magnificent Cork Oak, *Quercus suber*. The bark is so deeply fissured, fingers disappear deep into its spongy crevices and one horizontal bough stretches some sixty feet, from the base of the tree.

From here I am instinctively drawn to the far end of the *Magnolia grandiflora* avenue, to find out what lies beneath a small turreted gazebo. A short walk reveals it to be just about the largest bell imaginable. This is the famous Mandalay Bell, brought back to Antony from Burma by General Sir Reginald Pole-Carew in 1886. Alongside leans an ancient, moss covered, Field Maple, *Acer campestre* and an even older, but flourishing, Mulberry, *Morus nigra* which has decided it is easier to lay gently alongside the path, rather than struggle to maintain the perpendicular. The path leads on around the outside of a walled garden, the soft, pock marked, red brickwork partially hidden by espalier fruit including peaches, pears and plums. At their base is a stunning collection of day lilies, *Hemerocallis* assembled by the late Lady Cynthia

Carew-Pole in the 1960's and 1970's. With over 500 varieties Antony now holds the National Collection. A lovely Maidenhair Tree, *Ginkgo biloba* stands sentry like, guarding the gateway which leads into a formal arrangement of smaller gardens, each enclosed by a mixture of yew hedging and garden wall. One walks between these gardens like passing through the rooms of a house. This intimate, almost secretive, part of the garden, has been designed and created by the present Lady Carew-Pole and has an atmosphere that is quite different from the rest of the garden. The first 'room' has a sundial for a central feature, which is surrounded by quartered, lavender bordered herbaceous beds, deliberately planted for scent with a delightful array of roses and Mock Orange, *Philadelphus*. To one side sits a wheelbarrow bench, iron wheel at one end, wooden handles at the other, just ready to be wheeled into the required position, be it sun or shade. I step through a doorway cut into the yew hedging which takes me into the summer knot garden. Here an intricate design of closely clipped box hedging is best viewed from one of the two wooden corner seats, cleverly constructed to allow visitors a bird's eye view of the garden. Each 'room' is quite different and full of surprises, not least the recently introduced metal sculpture known as 'Hypercone'. Designed by Simon Thomas in 1996, it creates interesting shadows, which creep across the verdant manicured lawns before the sun gets high in the sky. Turning away from 'Hypercone' one's attention is drawn to two young pears, *Pyrus nivalis*, which are absolutely smothered with pure white blossom from tip to toe and against the garden wall, one of my favourite large shrubs, the Pineapple Broom, *Cytisus battandieri*. When in flower in early summer the sweet, fruity fragrance from its bright yellow blooms cannot be bettered.

On leaving the intimacy of the garden 'rooms', I suddenly find myself in an area of the main garden which almost defies description it is so breathtakingly beautiful. I am walking beneath an avenue of *Magnolia denudata*, the Lily Tree, in full flower. Leafless, twisted branches reach out far above my head, bedecked with literally hundreds of great, white goblet shaped flowers. The ground beneath the avenue is littered with fallen sepals which adds to the feeling that one is walking down a long white tunnel, at the end of which glows the fresh, bronzy-orange, emerging foliage of a Pride of India, *Koelreuteria paniculata*. Where the magnolia blossom ends, pear blossom begins, contrasting dramatically against the red brick of the old garden wall. Basking in the warmth radiating from the wall are many tender plants including *Acacia pravissima*, *Sophora tetraptera*, *Callistemon bigiou*, *Fremontodendron californicum* and *Holboellia latifolia* which produces wonderful purple female and yellow male flowers on the plant at the same time.

I head northwards from here and enter the Woodland Garden by the Garden Field gate. Covering almost 60 acres, the Woodland Garden, or Wilderness as it is so called, is run by the Carew-Pole Garden Trust.

Crossing the Garden Field between superb drifts of daffodils, interspersed with several splendid Himalayan Birch, *Betula utilis*, I follow a grassy track towards Higher Westdown Wood. The views of the woodland from the grounds around the house had given nothing away and in truth I entered the wood with little expectation. It wasn't long however before I began to realise that what I had seen of Antony up to now was only the beginning, just a taste of greater things to come. Groups of pink, white and red flowered camellias almost hurried down the banks to greet me. *Camellia japonica* 'Margaret Rose', named after Princess Margaret, *Camellia x williamsii* 'Brigadoon' with large rose-pink blooms and *Camellia* 'Anticipation' were just three of the first wave. It seemed every step brought into view at least half a dozen more, until I was literally walking through a camellia forest. The ground on my right began to drop away into a steep narrow valley, in the bottom a little stream burbled and gurgled its way down to the Lynher. Camellias swept on past me right down to the stream side, their blooms above me, below me, indeed all around me and beneath my feet great swathes of wild garlic in full flower played like surf across the valley sides. Gradually the camellias began to give way to other spring flowering shrubs including the delightful *Rhododendron williamsianum* with its shell-pink bell like flowers and heart shaped, chocolate coloured young leaves and high above my head giant tree magnolias, *sprengeri* and *campbellii* swayed gently in the salt laden breeze drifting in from the estuary.

Higher Westdown Wood has to be one of the loveliest woodland dells in Cornwall, if not England. The further one walks, the more beautiful the dell becomes. In places specimen plants grown for their foliage such as *Metasequoia glyptostroboides* and *Nothofagus dombeyi* intermingle with spring flowering shrubs and all around the woodland floor is covered with bluebells, primroses, violets and wild garlic. I pause beneath an enormous *Magnolia x veitchii* in full flower, the scent is intoxicating, drawing bees from miles around to collect its sweet nectar. Close by is the red barked *Rhododendron kewensi* and the majestic *Rhododendron macabeanum* with grey-felted leaves and delicate pale lemon flowers. I could spend the rest of the day, indeed the week wandering through this wonderful dell but the smell of the salt in the air reminds me that there is still more to see and I head down the path towards the bank of the River Lynher. Along the way I pass a group of Russian Rock Birch, *Betula ermanii* with wonderful, pure white, shaggy peeling bark. Antony is without doubt, a plantsman's garden, there are plants here rarely seen outside Cornwall such as *Michelia doltsopa* and the superb *Myrtus lechleriana*. Yet at the same time its aesthetic appeal is such that those with little or no horticultural knowledge cannot fail to be moved by its sheer beauty.

The path climbs steeply alongside a small stream and a succession of ponds filled with water lilies. Here, in the heart of the Wilderness, Tree Rhododendrons of gigantic proportions clamber up the escarpment creating a spectacular floral curtain of colour. *Rhododendron arboreum* and *Rhododendron griffithianum*, their flower laden boughs almost touching the water, battle for supremacy alongside *Magnolia liliiflora* and the exquisitely beautiful, pale pink, thin petalled flowers of *Rhododendron schlippenbachii*. I stop at the top of the slope to take in the view. Spread out beneath my feet, like on some Himalayan mountainside, are flowering magnolias and rhododendrons of every shade imaginable from the purest white to the deepest red.

The way back from here winds through a dell of conifers which includes a superb Eastern Hemlock, *Tsuga canadensis*, a Westfelton Yew, *Taxus baccata* 'Dovastoniana' and that most primitive of all conifers the Maidenhair Tree, *Ginkgo biloba*. Shortly afterwards I arrive at the edge of the vast sloping lawn in front of Antony House.

During the whole of my time here I have seen just a handful of visitors, nevertheless it is not only those gardens that receive thousands and thousands of visitors a year that can be described as 'great'. Indeed, I can think of several in this category that, for me, are quite uninspiring. Great gardens should inspire, delight and even astound through skillful plant associations and colour combinations. They should have the ability to create an atmosphere, a spirit that lives on in the visitor long after he or she returns home, for me, Antony does all that and more. Since that first visit in 1995 I have returned several times, on each occasion I have had the grounds virtually to myself, which is in one way delightful but in another quite sad. Perhaps on my next visit there will be a few more people finding inspiration during their own voyage of discovery.

Opposite 24. Rhododendrons in the Woodland Wilderness

26. Hypercone sculpture by Simon Thomas

27. Watercone sculpture by William Pye

28. Topiary cone inspiration for the Watercone

29. Surrounding wall with roses

30. Intimate Japanese garden to east end of terrace

31. The Summer Garden

32/33. Profusion of wild flowers in the Higher Westdown Wood

34. View of the river Lynher with spring daffodils

35. Roses and catmint in the terrace border

36. The Knot Garden in the enclosed Summer Garden

Lanhydrock

Lanhydrock

Ask anyone, who has an interest in these things, to name a well known Cornish garden that is open to the public and the name that comes back time and time again is Lanhydrock. Even with the recent phenomenal interest in "lost gardens", Lanhydrock has maintained its position as one of the places to visit on any Cornish garden tour. This is hardly surprising when one considers it has been owned by the National Trust and open to the public since 1953 and has a long established reputation as a garden 'par excellence'.

Lanhydrock was the first Cornish garden I ever visited, close on thirty years ago, as a boy on holiday with my parents, staying in a small wooden chalet amongst the sand dunes of Hayle on the North Cornish coast. Why Lanhydrock, ... well in truth it probably had a lot to do with the fact that its name appeared more often on the local coach operators chalk board than anything other than Land's End and we did that last Tuesday. Besides, is a nice name, sounds a bit Welsh and of course we could go into the house if it rained. Sound familiar? ..... excursions on family holidays were sometimes planned like that and quite often still are. The interesting thing is, I cannot remember a thing about my day at Land's End but Lanhydrock stands out as the golden moment on that holiday. Other than Lorraine of course, the girl from Dudley staying in the blue weatherboard chalet we passed every morning as we trudged through the soft sand to get our milk and daily bread. On that holiday I discovered something that kindled a passion within me that is still there today. Something that did not come from Dudley, West Midlands, Lorraine found her passion with the boy who handed out pennies for change in an amusement arcade in St Ives. My passion came from much further afield, it came from the mist shrouded foothills of the Himalayas, the deep river gorges of Yunnan and the age old forests of Oregon. The homes of so many of the plants I saw about me.

The time rolled by and I did not return to Lanhydrock for at least ten years but then having returned, I fell in love with the place all over again and since then have become a frequent visitor. Brown tourist signs on the A30, just outside Bodmin, are a constant reminder, whenever one drives down the peninsular, of Lanhydrock's existence and once off the dual carriageway one enters a different world.

High banked country lanes covered with a seasonal succession of wild flowers from celandines to red campion lead one into a gravelled car park surrounded by mature beech woodland.

Just across the country lane, burr covered oaks line the drive leading to the house and church. To either side cattle graze placidly on open pasture, oblivious to the screeching hoards of swallows that skit around the oaks like gangs of young children excitedly playing tag in a playground.

The first glimpse of St Hydroc's grey turreted church tower, surrounded by rhododendrons and two splendid copper beeches, is quite lovely. It glides into view from behind an old heavy branched Monterey Pine, *Pinus radiata*, some of its giant broken limbs cast around its base. Soon after, the grey slate roof of the house, which is arranged on three sides of a central courtyard, can be seen nestling deep into a wooded hillside which rises some two hundred feet immediately behind. Catch it at the right time of the year and your heart will skip a beat, for this hillside will come alive with literally thousands of flowers from the rhododendrons, camellias, magnolias and azaleas which flourish in the rich, acid, loam soils that abound here. The mix of colours against a backdrop of fresh, lime-green beeches, standing proud on the skyline, is quite breathtaking, and it's up there, high on the hillside above Lanhydrock House that the real horticultural gems of this magnificent garden are waiting to be discovered.

The present house, other than the entrance porch and the north wing, is little more than one hundred years old, the original seventeenth-century property having been severely damaged by fire in 1881. It was given to the National Trust in 1953 by the seventh Viscount Clifden. Those who venture inside today, and it is really well worth visiting, will find a unique record of life in a Victorian country residence.

For me however, it is outside the house where the greatest excitement begins. There are wonderful formal gardens within the confines of Lanhydrock's castellated walls and they start immediately beyond the gatehouse. Here, on immaculate lawns, stand twenty-nine closely clipped, columnar, Irish Yews, *Taxus baccata* var. *fastigiata*, planted in 1857. Alongside, to emphasise the formality of this area, are a number of bronze urns complete with cherubs, brought here from the Château de Bagatelle in Paris. In between the yews are a series of rose beds, each planted up with a different variety including 'Margaret Merril', 'Escapade', 'Octavia Hill', 'Bright Smiles' and 'The Fairy'. On warm early summer days their fragrance is exquisite, drifting over the regularly clipped box hedging of the parterre, where a succession of plantings provides stunning colour displays from tulips in spring to

Previous pages 37. Early morning view of the house and parkland at Lanhydrock

begonias and impatiens in summer. The best view of the parterre is from the churchyard wall, which stands a terrace or two higher, and is approached via a short flight of stone steps at the end of the Church Border. Here electric blue agapanthus flower alongside fuchsias and clematis and an Albertine rose rambles and scrambles along a parapet, all but obscuring a small granite seat set deep into a cool stone recess.

The way to the upper gardens is through the wrought iron gates just above the parterre. Immediately outside are two superb Copper Beeches. They look as though they have been there for centuries, but were in fact planted by the Liberal Parliamentarians, William Gladstone and Lord Rosebery. Gladstone planting one on 18th June 1889, and Rosebery the other in November 1905. This part of Cornwall was, and still is, a Liberal stronghold. From here the grounds starts to rise and with it my sense of anticipation. To the right is the old croquet lawn and behind it, quite ironically in this garden of exotic plants from all over the temperate world, is the most fascinating, native, Field Maple, *Acer campestre*. It is absolutely smothered with mosses, lichen and polypody ferns, which thrive in Lanhydrock's clean, moist air and in spring, carpets of bluebells creep under its canopy right up to the ancient gnarled and twisted trunk. Close by, *Acer palmatum*, 'Sango Kaku' displays through spring and early summer the kind of leaf colour you would expect to see in October. Delightful apricot-coloured foliage carried on twigs that turn a coral-red as soon as the first frosts of winter arrive, truly a tree for all seasons. The first of many magnolias, *Magnolia delavayi* with its thick robust leaves and fragrant creamy-white flowers from mid-summer onwards, gives a taste of things to come and just beyond an arched iron gate leading to the higher garden, it is time to throw away the horticultural rule book and simply gaze in wonder at plants that really have no right to grow as big as they do at Lanhydrock.

In the spring head for the Veitchii Border where large magnolia blooms hang low over the churchyard wall and the narrow grass paths are full of wonderful fragrances from choice shrubs such as *Corylopsis glabrescens*, *Osmanthus burkwoodii* and the delightful bell shaped flowers of *Enkianthus campanulatus*. By early summer Mock Orange, *Philadelphus* and the Chinese Dogwood, *Cornus kousa* will hold centre stage for a while before giving way to the spectacular autumnal tints of *Acer japonicum* 'Aconitifolium' and the Persian Ironwood *Parottia persica* which draw such gasps of admiration from visitors in October. In truth, there are delights to be found in any season at Lanhydrock but as with most Cornish gardens it is the spring that dominates. The path from the

Veitchii Border to Borlase's stream passes beneath magnolia giants such as *Magnolia x veitchii* and *dawsoniana*, with blooms fifty feet or more off the ground. Whilst at eye-level look out for the giant banana-like leaves of *Magnolia ashei* and deep blackcurrant coloured flowers of *Magnolia liliiflora* 'Nigra' which flower well into summer.

One of my favourite spots at Lanhydrock is the fast flowing runnel known as Borlase's stream, which springs out from the hillside into a little dipping well, virtually hidden by a clump of Royal Fern, *Osmunda regalis*. From here the stream runs under the path and meanders down the slope in the direction of the house. Its passage is clearly evident from frothy plantings of astilbes, arum lilies, rodgersias and candelabra primulas which thrive in the fertile damp soils of the streamside. It is in this area that mist, which swirls down off the flanks of Bodmin moor, hangs the longest, deadening every sound except the stream, which seems to gurgle ever louder as the mist thickens. All around, massive colour-drained tree trunks drift in and out of view and a constant rain of camellia petals, made heavy by the moisture laden mist, fall steadily to the ground. Lanhydrock has many moods, but for me this is one of the most evocative. Stark, bare branches, illuminated by hundreds of glowing magnolia blooms, light the way down petal strewn paths and if the mist does turn to gentle rain, which it quite often does, there is always the old thatched gardener's cottage to take shelter in. This delightful cottage, last occupied in 1885, has decorated walls both inside and out. Carmine-pink flowers of *Camellia reticulata* 'Captain Rawes', hang in abundance from the south wall and inside, the whitewashed walls are covered with an array of agricultural tools and implements, including some very fearsome looking man traps above the door.

It is just a hop and a skip from here, through a yew hedge, into the Herbaceous Circle, the southern half of which was laid out by Lady Clifden just before the First World War. It is a must for any late spring or summer visitor. The circle is neatly quartered by grass paths over which spill fiery crocosmias, the wonderful pale orange, lily-like *Cardiocrinum giganteum* and in late summer *Sedum spectabile* 'Autumn Joy' which is easily found by following clouds of tortoiseshell butterflies. A nice touch here is the laminated bed plans, from which the plants can be readily identified, just as long as you know your points of the compass, the trick is to first check out where the sundial is positioned. The Herbaceous Circle is overlooked by a stone barn, built from the remains of an old monk's house and containing the former east window from the chancel of St Hydroc's church. An enormous Chinese

Gooseberry, *Actinidia chinensis* clambers over the barn, adjacent wall and an old Japanese Cherry. The superb fragrance from its creamy-white flowers with orange stamen centre, is quite intoxicating. Wherever I come across it, be it in a garden or garden centre, anywhere in the country, that first distinctive breath of perfume immediately transports me back to the Herbaceous Circle at Lanhydrock. Just outside is probably one of the loveliest of all flowering shrubs, *Deutzia x hybrida* 'Perle Rose', it has striking deep burgundy coloured buds which open to reveal beautiful pale, blush-pink flowers, definitely one of my top ten shrubs! From here the path leads upwards past The Long Border where hostas, hypericums and day lilies flank the path, behind which are several stunning specimens of *Osmanthus delavayi* and *Hydrangea aspera*.

At the end of The Long Border, set in a decorative stone well house, is the Holy Well, said to have been used by the monks of St Petroc's Priory. The water inside is deep and clear, coins glisten and glint far beneath the shimmering surface which is disturbed by a steady trickle of water from the hill behind. At this point I am never sure which way to go first, for the delights now come thick and fast in every direction. Broad path is a spectacular promenade between vibrant coloured walls of flower from the scores of giant rhododendrons planted along its length. Here and there, spaces in the planting reveal dramatic views of the house, parkland and the avenue rolling eastwards towards Fowey. In the immediate foreground one looks down onto a magnificent array of mature trees including the soft, feathery foliage of both the Swamp Cypress, *Taxodium distichum*, and the Dawn Redwood, *Metasequoia glyptostroboides*. Having taken in this marvellous vista, head back towards the Holy Well and then turn left beneath what is undoubtedly one of Lanhydrock's finest features, The Magnolia Tunnel. An iron archway winds its way up the hill, upon which rests ancient bonsai like boughs of *Magnolia soulangeana* 'Lennei' and *Magnolia soulangeana* 'Rustica Rubra'. In spring their goblet-shaped blooms completely cover the arch, producing a tunnel of flowers. To walk through on a sunny May morning with carpets of bluebells on either side is an experience never to be forgotten. It is from here that I find myself leaving the path every few yards, plunging deep into the undergrowth to discover yet another Lanhydrock special. On emerging from the tunnel, one of the first gems is a superb Chinese Dogwood, *Cornus kousa*, and standing opposite a gigantic *Magnolia hypoleuca*, some sixty feet tall, with creamy-white blossoms right to the highest branch. Next comes a wonderful group of trees specially chosen for their attractive bark, including the Paperbark

Maple, *Acer griseum*, Tibetan Cherry, *Prunus serrula*, and Snake Bark Maple, *Acer forestii*. Beyond stands a magnificent Brewers Spruce, *Picea breweriana*, its long, weeping, evergreen foliage hanging gracefully through a Japanese Rowan, *Sorbus discolor*, 'Joseph Rock' which will be at its best in late summer when it provides bunches of golden-amber berries.

If you plan to visit Lanhydrock for the first time, try to get there when the deciduous azaleas are in flower. On a warm, sunny morning the sight and scent of their stunning flower displays is quite remarkable and worth every step of the journey up the hill from the house. Just when you think you must have seen it all, if you are very lucky, which I have been only once, you may catch the Foxglove Trees, *Paulownia tomentosa* in flower. High on the hillside, way above the house, they stand proud and majestic, like kings looking down on their subjects. They have tall, lilac-purple spikes of flowers, up to twelve inches long. Closer inspection will reveal each flower to be almost orchid-like in design, their individual orange-speckled throat a cavern of delight for bumble bees. Without doubt they are part of the aristocracy of the flower world.

Towards the end of the Top Path just before the exotic plantings start to give way to native woodland, is a delightful thatched cob summerhouse. Erected in 1993, it commemorates the work done by Lanhydrock's gardeners, in particular Head Gardener Peter Borlase, to rectify the damage caused by the devastating storms of January 1990. I truly love this place, which I always make my last stop on any visit to Lanhydrock. It has wonderful views across the valley towards Caradon Hill to the south-east of Bodmin Moor. To sit here surrounded by the cream of trees and shrubs, collected from all around the temperate world over the last one hundred years, is an emotional experience not just for gardeners and foresters, but for anyone who has an appreciation of the beauty found both within this garden and in the wider undulating landscape of the parkland beyond. From here, those leaving the grounds and making their way up the drive to the entrance pavilion, are clearly visible.

Like me, you may first arrive at Lanhydrock knowing nothing more than its name. I guarantee when you leave, that name will be synonymous with a treasured memory that will bring you back time and time again.

Opposite 38. The parterre with tulips and forget-me-nots

39. St. Hydroc's church from the parterre

40. *Albertine* roses by stone steps

41. *Ceanothus* in front of house

42. Parterre with summer flowering *Begonias*

43. Early summer view of house and parkland

44. The church of Saint Hydroc

45. Spring view of house and parkland

46. Churchyard border in late spring

47. Church outer wall

48. Fallen rhododendron petals on Top Path

49. Borlase's stream through the Higher Garden

50. Bluebells and red campion in the wood

51. Bluebells and azaleas close to the West Path

52. View through to The Gatehouse

53. Framed rhododendron

54. View from the churchyard to Church Path

55. Herbaceous circle in Circular Garden

56. *Acer palmatum* 'Sango Kaku' by the Croquet Lawn

57. View of The Gatehouse and the main house

48

58. Old thatched gardeners cottage in the Higher Garden

59. *Magnolia campbellii* with mist rolling in from Bodmin Moor

60. Misty camellia and magnolia petals in the Higher Garden

61. Winding path through the Higher Garden

62. *Camellia japonica*

63. *Camellia japonica*

64. *Camellia japonica*

65. *Camellia japonica* 'Lady Clare'

66. *Camellia x williamsii* 'Glenn's Orbit'

67. *Camellia japonica* 'Lady Clare'

68. Tulip 'China Pink' with forget-me-nots

69. Tulip 'West Point' with forget-me-nots

70. View from the parterre to the Croquet Lawn

51

Heligan

The Lost Gardens of Heligan

There can be few people in Britain who have not heard of Heligan. From its 'discovery' in 1990, until the completion of the Sundial Garden restoration in 1996, Heligan has received more publicity than any other garden in Britain. Quite early on, The Times described Heligan as "the garden restoration of the century". That was before the best selling book, the Channel Four television series and the video. The story of how Tim Smit and John Nelson hacked their way into the garden using machetes, has already become part of gardening folklore. As has *that* photograph, who wouldn't have wanted to push that door open, just to see what was on the other side? The difference is, most of us would have looked in wonderment and then walked away. Tim and John looked and fell in love with what they saw. Not only that, they looked and saw beyond the entangled wilderness and rotting timber-framed greenhouses. In short they possessed vision. Over the last eight years, through courage, doggedness and boundless enthusiasm they have managed to turn their vision into reality. In Tim's own words, "it was a case of: the rest of your life starts here. Madness? Folly even. Few people are privileged to have such adventures. None of us would have missed it for the world".

You can look at Heligan in one of two ways. The first is the purist approach. Perhaps 'asleep for seventy years' is stretching the point somewhat, perhaps Heligan doesn't possess the greatest plant collection in Cornwall, perhaps, at times, the gardens have struggled to keep pace with the hype. Or, you can take the romantic approach; there is no other garden in the world quite like Heligan; it provides an opportunity for all of us to step back in time; the restoration of Heligan really is history in the making. Looked at individually, there is probably some truth in all of these statements, but what is more important is the whole. Heligan is an experience, an adventure, waiting for your arrival. Once there you must allow the chains to fall from your imagination. There is a spirit, a magical quality to the place, but it will only touch you if you allow it. To unlock those chains just remember two things. One hundred years ago there was a great garden, just eight years ago there was a wilderness.

I have explored Heligan three times in the last three years. Once on my own, once with a friend and once in the company of John Nelson. I have been there in the early morning, when rhododendron blooms hung heavy with dew. I have been there in the evening, when the last rays of the sun have set fire to the golden-cinnamon coloured bark of myrtle trees close to the Flower Garden. I have been there after a summer rainstorm, when the heat from the emerging sun has filled The Jungle with great humid, clouds of vapour. Each time I visit I discover new plants, new paths, new locations and at times, I have felt like the first person to explore some tucked away path for years, if not decades.

As you arrive, think of your visit as an exploration, a journey of discovery through uncharted territory. My explorations of Heligan have always started from the cluster of wooden buildings, which make up the entrance area. No plush, grand entry pavilion to this garden. Quite the opposite, it has almost a temporary, shanty town feel to it. The buildings huddle together, as if for safety, in a clearing hacked from the jungle. Having passed through the clearing, one enters a dark tunnel of evergreen foliage, cut through an over-mature, shelter belt of laurel. There is a sign at this point which says, 'beware of low-hanging branches'. Nothing like stating the obvious, even the casual visitor will find themselves ducking from time to time and the plantsman will forever be diving through thickets and dense leafy bowers, like some Victorian plant collector on a first trip to the Himalayas. I emerge from the tunnel into bright sunshine and the Lost Garden beyond. The transformation is striking, bird song reverberates from the tops of stag-headed old oaks, and the humming of bees is quite thunderous from within creamy-white flower trumpets of a tree rhododendron high above my head. Before me stretches a flat, grassy, open area bordered on all sides by rhododendrons of immense proportions. This is Flora's Green, known as such because it is reputed that Cornish floral dancing took place here. Crossing the centre of the green, I make my way towards a small, evergreen tree, covered in what looks from a distance like a great cloud of sulphur-yellow, Brimstone butterflies. The tree is *Cornus capitata*, Bentham's Cornel, originally from the Himalayas and Western China, and the yellow is actually hundreds of bracts, protective sheaths, surrounding small, dense flower heads. The effect is quite stunning, and later in the year, these flowers will turn into large, red strawberry-like fruits. Heligan was one of the very first gardens in the country to grow *Cornus capitata*, as far back as 1822. In later years, whole avenues of them lined the length of the Main Ride, what a superb sight that must have been.

Wherever possible I leave the path, to explore the thick clumps of vegetation on either side. Here one finds age old fallen tree trunks, with great upturned root plates, which play host to micro gardens as diverse

Previous pages 71. The Jungle. The Lost Garden of Heligan

as the grounds they once stood in. Bracket fungus, seedling rhododendrons, garlands of ivy, buttercups, primroses and great fleshy-leaved foxglove rosettes, all grow out of the nutrient rich, mossy remains of these fallen logs. Indeed, in this garden of secrets, there are as many horizontal woody plants as vertical ones. Not just the result of decades of neglect, many came crashing down only days before Tim Smit and John Nelson made their first sortie into the grounds. Seven hundred and thirty nine trees fell here on the night of the great storm of 24th January 1990. It was as if the gardens knew this was their last chance to ensure no human being ever set foot inside again.

Breaking cover, my attention is drawn to a white dovecote complete with guardian owl post. It stands in the shadow of a giant *Magnolia campbellii*, which is still bearing one or two large pink, sprawling blooms amongst rapidly expanding fleshy green leaves. On all sides of the magnolia, enormous rhododendrons press in, including *Rhododendron sinogrande*, which has massive leaves, up to eighteen inches long, curved on the underside with a soft, fawn-coloured down, known as indumentum.

Following the gardens northern boundary one eventually comes to the Northern Summerhouse, where one gets the occasional glimpse of Mevagissey Bay. At the turn of the century this must have been a wonderful spot. The Summerhouse is probably the oldest building in the garden, being clearly marked on a plan of 1770. It was in the late 1800's however that a hedge of laurel was planted and then clipped to form three viewing windows through the foliage, which looked out across the bay. It wasn't until late in 1991 that the Summerhouse was re-discovered, almost by chance. The story goes that John Nelson's dog went missing, whilst a team of Heligan staff and volunteers were trying to clear around the northern boundary. Suddenly excited barking from the dog, drew the team even deeper into the undergrowth, whereupon they found the dog standing excitedly in the front of one of three red brick arches, the entrance to an old summerhouse. The roof and remains of a wooden bench seat that had once lined the walls, lay rotting on the floor. Once this was cleared the floor was found to be of a lovely brick and cobble design. The summerhouse was restored to its former glory by the following Easter, just in time for the official opening of the Lost Gardens of Heligan to the public on April 17th 1992.

From the northern Summerhouse you can go one of two ways, down into the dank, magical, shady area known as New Zealand or on past an enormous *Rhododendron* 'Cornish Red' and along the northern boundary of the Vegetable Garden. I choose the latter and enter the Vegetable Garden through an opening in a recently planted cypress hedge. The view from this point is quite amazing. Uniform rows of summer vegetables and soft fruit run away southwards into the distance. Either side of the main path, which dissects the area into two, are great colourful swathes of flowering antirrhinums and sweet william. In this enclosed garden, as the sun warms up the soil, there is a wonderful mixture of fragrances. Sweet william scent intermingles with that from great heaps of rich, salty seaweed piled around the asparagus beds and from the warm brown earth surrounding a freshly dug potato patch. Overhead, a breeze clatters together the rigid fronds of a line of Chusan Palms, *Trachycarpus fortunei* which stand just outside the garden. It seems strange, almost bizarre to look up from this very English, Edwardian landscape of the vegetable garden to the exotic foliage of the palms above. Celery, celeric, chard, (Swiss and Ruby), Jerusalem artichokes ten feet tall, globe artichokes, cabbage as big as footballs, whatever the vegetable you will find it here and quite probably its name too. Such wonderful names of the old varieties that would have been growing on this spot at the turn of the century, include old potato varieties such as 'Ninety Fold', 'Rycroft Purple', Edzell Blue'. As I wander down the straight functional paths, I fully expect to meet, at any moment, an Edwardian head gardener, perhaps ticking off the gardener's boy for planting just one pea slightly out of line.

The path leads on from the Vegetable Garden, beneath old iron hoops supporting young grafted espalier apples and lines of flowering sweet peas, into the Melon Yard. Here, gooseberries are trained some six feet tall up the old red brick wall and around their base are lashings of strawberries and terracotta forcing pots. After years of dereliction it is a delight to see, once again, melons, pineapples and cucumbers, growing beneath brilliant white, wooden-framed glass-houses. The pineapple pit is reported to be the only one working and actually growing pineapples in Britain. The achievements at Heligan over the past eight years are many, but for me the finest has to be the restoration of these productive gardens and glass-houses. In its heyday, the Heligan estate was self-sufficient in just about everything except coal and lime. These gardens would have provided all the fruit, vegetables, herbs, cut flowers and other ornamentals for the house. Even honey was provided from bee boles, wicker skeps set within recesses in the garden wall. However, the days of such productivity on estates throughout Britain were drawing to a close. Already the guns were massing on the Western Front.

In the corner of the Melon Yard is a little bothy. This is where the gardener's boy would sleep, getting up regularly to check the temperature in the glass-houses and to ensure the manure wasn't about to spontaneously combust. Inside this small room, the boy slept on a wooden floor, suspended just above head height, his bed just sacking and straw. Beneath were two white-washed cubicles, each containing thunderboxes for use by the garden staff. These boxes would have been emptied elsewhere and their contents used as manure. Written into the plaster of one of these cubicles with lead pencil are the words "come ye not here to sleep nor slumber". Beneath is written the names of all the gardeners of the day. The date, August 1914. Twenty two names in all, by 1918 all had enlisted, more than half died on the muddy fields of Flanders and few ever returned. This was the start of Heligan's decline.

Beyond the Melon Yard lies the high, red bricked wall of the Flower Garden. Entry into this garden is through the door, pushed open by Tim and John on February 16th 1990. Although flowers were certainly grown here, so were also many tender vegetables as it is the most sheltered of all the gardens. Around the perimeter, against the warm walls, pears, cherries and apples would have been grown in addition to the fruit within the citrus, vine and peach-houses. Today this garden is once again becoming as productive as it would have been during the last century. It is well worth spending a few minutes looking at the before and after photographs on the wall. They give just some idea of the incredible restoration work that has gone on here over the last eight years.

I could spend all day wandering around these productive gardens, there is so much to see, so much of interest. In a little corner of the Flower Garden, close to the Citrus House is a lovely collection of fuchsias. All varieties that were available before 1910 and would have been at the disposal of Heligan's head gardener.

The last garden to be restored was the Sundial Garden, it was not completed until 1996. It lies directly to the south of the Flower Garden and has a wonderful herbaceous border running away to a super *Davidia involucrata*, Pocket Handkerchief Tree in the far distance. In 1896 this garden was described in 'Gardeners Chronicle' as having "the finest herbaceous border in England". Although in its infancy today, it does have the potential to one day re-capture this marvellous accolade.

Beyond the Sundial Garden is private ground surrounding Heligan House. I make my way back through the Sundial Garden admiring on the way some *daturas* in large wooden planters, let out of the greenhouses for summer, by October they will be safely back behind glass.

Such is the diversity of Heligan's many gardens, that just a few minutes walk from the formality of the walled gardens, one can be standing amidst just about the most exotic landscape on mainland Britain. The Jungle Garden is a steep-sided, sub-tropical valley garden incorporating four interconnecting ponds. It is such a thrilling experience to push through rampant, lush vegetation which is clambering from the water margins up the valley sides to greet each intrepid explorer. One really does feel that civilisation has been left far behind and who knows what native tribe may be lying in wait just around the next corner. Down here, far below the house, there are bamboos, palms and tree ferns, plus the tallest *Podocarpus totara*, New Zealand Totara Tree, in Britain. Boardwalks traverse both sides of the jungle, it is literally the only way to move around down here, leave them at your peril, you may never come out alive. Occasionally, between gigantic leaves of *Gunnera manicata* across the valley, just the face will appear of another intrepid visitor, the rest of their body and indeed that of those accompanying them will be completely hidden from view by the luxuriant vegetation. The effect is quite unnatural, almost surreal, especially on hot humid days when great clouds of vapour hang in the valley.

I said earlier, Heligan is an experience, an adventure waiting for your arrival. I guarantee a walk through the jungle garden is an experience you will never forget.

From here the only way out is back up the steep winding path to the formal gardens to the north of the house. There is still so much to see, the Italian Garden, the Ravine, the Grotto, 'New Zealand' and I haven't even had an afternoon cup of tea. I make my way back to the safety of the shanty town and some refreshment. On the way I pass two, well dressed, middle-aged ladies deep in conversation, 'well I didn't know what to expect, it certainly is different, but I'm so glad I came, I must tell Joyce and George – I know they will love it".

Opposite 72. Magnificent *Rhododendron* 'Cornish Red' in The Jungle

73. The Italian Garden

74. The Italian Garden

75. The Italian Garden

76. The Italian Garden

77. The Melon Garden

78. The Wishing Well

79. The Sundial Garden

80. Herbaceous border on The Ride

82. Sweet William in the Vegetable Garden

81. Vegetables on parade

83. Agave in The Italian Garden

84. Parrot Tulip in The Italian Garden

85. *Camellia* petals in The Italian Garden

86. Sweet William in The Vegetable Garden

87. Iris in the pool in The Italian Garden

88. Lacecap *Hydrangeas* with *Astilbes* on The Ride

90. The Jungle with Tree Ferns *Dicksonia antarctica*
and Skunk Cabbage *Lysichiton americanus*

89. Deep in The Jungle with *Rhododendron* 'Cornish
Red' and Chusan Palm *Trachycarpus fortunei*

91. Group of Tree Ferns *Dicksonia antarctica* in The Jungle

92. Lush summer greens across The Jungle

93. Fallen tree in The Lost Valley

Caerhays

Caerhays Castle Garden

There can be few gardens in Britain with a more romantic setting than that of Caerhays Castle on the south Cornwall coast just to the west of Mevagissey. It is approached from Porthluney Cove, a secluded south facing sun trap, where the sea breaks on silver grained sand surrounded by towering granite cliffs. The castle gatehouse is literally a stone's throw from the beach and once inside the grounds open out before you. One's eye initially settles on a small lake in the foreground but it is the baronial castle beyond that commands attention. It looks like a possible contender to stage the investiture of the next Prince of Wales, with its profusion of battlements, turrets and towers. In fact it is less than 200 years old, built in 1807 by none other than John Nash, the architect of Buckingham Palace and the Brighton Pavilion. It was commissioned by John Bettesworth Trevanion M.P. and was without doubt the most extravagant act by a member of the Trevanion family since they first settled in this remote corner of Cornwall in 1390. So extravagant in fact that the family were bankrupted and in 1840 forced to emigrate to Paris where John Bettesworth Trevanion died shortly afterwards.

The castle lay neglected until 1853 when a Cornish tin mine owner, Michael Williams, purchased the estate. He began to restore the castle to its original glory, work that was carried on by his son, John Michael Williams until his death in 1880. It was the third generation of Williams', John Charles Williams M.P., otherwise known as J.C. Williams, who first looked over the parapet and decided it was about time something was done with the garden. This almost flippant event was probably, as it turned out, the most important thing to happen at Caerhays since the creation of the castle more than 70 years before. It was to be the germination of a gardener in a man who would have the most profound influence on British horticulture. "J.C." gave up parliamentary life, turned his back on London society and in 1896 started a garden diary, determined to record every planting, every horticultural and meteorological event that took place during the development of his garden.

Like so many other keen gardeners at the end of the last century, J.C. soon caught the excitement generated by the opening up of China to the West and the deluge of new plant introductions being made by the great British plant collectors, in particular E.H. Wilson. Wilson's first expedition to China in 1900, financed by the Chelsea nurserymen, James Veitch and Sons, produced more than 1,500 packets of seeds of different plants, most of which had never been grown in Britain before. Almost half were rhododendrons and knowing how well suited the Cornish climate was for rhododendron growing, J.H. Veitch asked J.C. Williams to grow some of them at Caerhays. This request was greeted with great enthusiasm.

The first rhododendrons were big enough to be planted out in the castle grounds in 1905/06 and some of these, such as *Rhododendron lutescens* are still in existence today. By 1910 plant material was arriving at Caerhays from another great plant collector, the Scotsman George Forrest. Forrest was to spend over twenty years introducing plants from Yunnan Province in Western China. Camellias, magnolias, michelias, oaks and maples became regular entries in "J.C.'s" diary alongside the ever present rhododendrons. Once plants were safely established within the castle grounds, which was no easy task in the first place, many requiring careful siting, shelter and constant attention from Caerhays head gardeners, "J.C." would begin to practice his great passion for hybridisation. During the period 1910 until his death in 1939, he introduced to cultivation numerous hybrids of both rhododendron and magnolia including the very long flowering *Rhododendron* 'Crossbill', which is a cross between *Rhododendron lutescens* and *Rhododendron spinuliferum*. Many of these hybrids are firm favourites with gardeners throughout the world. However it is without doubt his work with camellias for which he is most revered. In 1925 he crossed *Camellia japonica* with *Camellia saluenensis* producing a hybrid which took its vigour and characteristic handsome polished leaves from *japonica* and exquisite flowers, produced in such profusion, from *saluenensis*. This hybrid is called *Camellia x williamsii*, it is one of the most valuable hybrids shrubs ever produced and without doubt the best camellia to grow in Britain. From this cross innumerable cultivars have been produced including 'Anticipation', 'Bow Bells' and 'Donation'.

After "J.C.'s" death, his eldest son Charles ensured the future of the collection, followed by his nephew, Julian Williams C.B.E. who appointed Philip Tregunna as Head Gardener, only the third Head Gardener since the creation of the gardens in 1896. Both are still there today, (although Philip officially retired in 1996, passing on the title of Head Gardener to Jaimie Parsons) and both are supremely proud and rightly so, of the parts they have played in ensuring that Caerhays enters the 21st century in the way that "J.C." would have wanted.

It was with Philip that I first explored the gardens of Caerhays Castle and I remember the occasion vividly.

Previous pages 94. Caerhays Castle to the sea

There was the castle, positively glistening as the sun picked out every quartz crystal within its grey granite walls, cradled above and to each side by a horseshoe of brilliant colours. Fold upon fold of red, pink, orange, yellow, cream and white cascading down the rhododendron clad hillside like some marauding band of pirates about to overrun the castle walls. Above it all, both in character and stature, stood the Asian magnolias, which even from some three hundred yards away could be seen to dwarf mature oaks and sycamores. I slowly walked closer, determined to remember every detail, so in years to come I could relate to others, not only every colour combination on the hillside but also the profound emotional experience that had so unexpectedly overtaken me. I was truly on hallowed ground, here in what could be thought of as one of the cradles of modern horticulture and I felt "J.C." was watching me, making sure my intentions were honourable.

Philip, guide map in hand, was waiting for me inside the castle courtyard, a softly spoken, gentle faced man. We climbed this steep path away from the castle and within a matter of minutes the last of its castellated walls had completely disappeared from view. It was at this point that Philip gave me some invaluable advice, "don't just look straight ahead, look up, look down, look to the sides and then back along the way you have just come', by then we were already deep within the woodland canopy. Gazing through the wood at eye level the trunks of the larger trees could easily have been mature beech or sycamore. It was only when I allowed my eyes to climb theses trees that the stunning truth struck home. For these mighty trunks were magnolias of immense proportions and right at their tops, set against an azure blue Cornish sky, were masses upon masses of lax petalled gigantic magnolia blooms ranging in colour from pure white to cerise. *Magnolia campbellii, sargentiana, sprengeri* and *x veitchii*, I had read all their vital statistics in my copy of 'Champion Trees of Britain' before visiting Caerhays and that was impressive enough but to see them at first hand was an experience like no other. They regularly topped seventy feet with trunks more than three feet in diameter and where they grew in sunlight on the edge of a glade, tea plate size flowers reached to the ground, to intermingle with pale lemon primroses, creating the choicest of bridal wreaths.

When the deciduous magnolias first arrived in Britain around the turn of the century they caused quite a stir, for they flower before the leaves emerge, which at that time was something rarely seen on plants in Britain. Believe it or not many people disapproved, feeling this to be quite a vulgar display and only planted those magnolias which flowered on branches modestly covered with leaves. Today, not only at Caerhays, but throughout the country, the flowering of the deciduous magnolias is considered a glorious spectacle and a sure sign that spring has arrived.

One of the special things about Caerhays is its topography. It is such a thrill to be able to stand on a bank and look down onto the tops of certain trees rather than always craning one's neck skywards. This is especially true with the magnolias. As Philip and I climbed slowly up the escarpment the flowers on such giants which just a few minutes before had seemed far beyond any closer inspection, were suddenly just inches away. One could almost touch each individual sepal and breathe in their heady fragrance, even though the roots of the tree on which they grew might be some eighty feet below.

So taken was I with the magnolias that it was very easy to miss some of the other choice plants that Caerhays has to offer and so it fell to Philip, as we made our way up onto the Main Ride, to stop and point some of these out. Tree Ferns *Dicksonia antarctica* from Australia, Tasmania and New Zealand, the Himalayan Tanbark Oak, *Lithocarpus pachyphyllus* and the lovely Nikko Maple, *Acer maximowiczianum*, a native of Japan and central China where it has become very rare indeed, to name just three.

The whole garden covers some sixty acres and even in March and April at the height of the Cornish spring flowering season it has a peaceful, tranquil atmosphere. Curving paths lead off in different directions, wild bird song abounds and occasionally the mewing call of a male peacock echoes up the valley, as like some park warden on patrol he struts around the castle walls. The higher we climb the more open the planting becomes, with few mature trees giving shelter to the hundreds of camellias that clothe this area. Already affected by drought and Dutch Elm Disease, on the night of January 25th 1990 so the great storm struck. Over two hundred large trees were lost from the gardens immediately behind the castle and another seven hundred from the surrounding woodland. In the words of Julian Williams, "the trees crushed all the plants on which they fell, the mess was indescribable." As Philip and I wander through this area, it is clear that although all the visible signs of damage have been removed the scars still remain, many of them in the sorrowful eyes of Philip himself. Foresters and gardeners are by their nature realists, they know that their creations are living entities and as such are subject to the same natural forces as any dynamic collection. However, having said all that, on the morning after the storm as Philip began to painstakingly assess every inch of damage, he knew in his heart, that a chapter in the history of Caerhays had been closed and that things would never be quite the same again.

It is no surprise considering the long relationship between Caerhays and camellias that a large proportion of the latest ornamental plantings are camellias and in many cases progeny from the originals. By early April the flowering season for many is over, species such as *Camellia saluenensis* and *Camellia x williamsii* were at their best in January. Nevertheless, such is the range at Caerhays that there are still a number just reaching perfection. *Camellia japonica* 'Alba Simplex' with its large, single white flowers and 'poached egg' centre of golden yellow stamens is quite magnificent, as is *Camellia* 'Dream Castle', it has such a profusion of shell-pink frilly blooms that the branches are weighed down to the ground. Camellia 'Brigadoon', one of the later cultivars produced from "J.C.'s" *Camellia x williamsii* hybrid stands some eight feet tall and has delightful, robust rose-pink flowers. Considering it was only planted in 1991, its size and vigour is tremendous.

Over the years there have been many plant cultivars given the name Caerhays and as Philip and I approach the top of the ridge, probably one of the finest comes into view, *Magnolia campbellii* 'Caerhays Surprise'. This superb magnolia produces flowers that in bud are so deeply coloured the nearest description can only be blackcurrant, gradually turning to the richest pink imaginable as the flowers open. It is for sure quite a climb from the castle up to this spot, shown on the map as simply 'George's Hut', but I would not have missed it for the world. In spring it is quite simply so beautiful it is almost dream-like. Whichever way one turns the foreground is just awash with colour. Up here magnolias, camellias, rhododendrons, azaleas and cherries combine to create the ultimate flowering spectacle, the crowning glory for the castle far below. Yet there is still more, for at this point one is reminded of Caerhays' close proximity to the Cornish coast. From here the view now opens up and for the first time since leaving the castle gatehouse, Porthluney Cove and the sea beyond come into view. For Philip it is a prospect experienced daily for almost 40 years, yet even he is happy to linger for a moment or two before we head off in search of one particular plant I had expressed a wish to see in flower. I do not have to wait long before my wish is granted, following Philip's pointing hand I can see tree some thirty feet tall, which from a distance looks like a white radiating sphere against the blue sky. *Michelia doltsopa*, a tender, semi-evergreen tree from Yunnan, Tibet and the eastern Himalayas,

introduced into Britain in 1918 by George Forrest. Even before we reach the tree I can smell the sweet, almost honey like fragrance of its creamy white flowers and once under its canopy the combination of this wonderful scent and the sound from hundreds of industrious bees collecting nectar is totally intoxicating. Those flowers not yet open are protected, in bud, by a golden treacle coloured soft felt covering, those already open stand proud of leathery, olive green leaves.

We drop down off the crest of the hill and plunge through great tunnels of laurel emerging close to an old quarry to the north of the castle. Here *Rhododendron lutescens* grows wild, freely seeding itself up the dark, dank quarry walls from where its primrose-yellow flowers shine like beacons. These are seedlings from the original introduction, collected by E.H. Wilson in China and sent to Caerhays from Veitch's nursery in 1904. As we leave the old quarry, the hissing sound of surf breaking on the beach in Porthluney Cove can be easily heard. A unique sound within a garden, even for Cornwall, but that's what Caerhays is, completely unique. The combination of its coastal location, undulating topography, mild climate, sheer scale and incredible plant collection is quite simply beyond duplication.

Shortly afterwards we enter the castle walls through a granite archway below the battlements over which a *Wisteria sinensis* runs amok. A series of grassy terraces lead down to the back of the castle. Each terrace is covered with a floral patchwork quilt of *Primulas*, their colours ranging from native pale lemon to deep burgundy, interspersed with daffodils and wild cyclamen. Outside the large wooden castle doors, themselves surrounded by waterfalls of colour from wall trained *Camellias* some twenty feet tall, I say goodbye to Philip Tregunna. "Oh, there is just one last thing you might be interested in," he quietly suggests, "that *Camellia japonica* by your right shoulder is the one Mr J.C. Williams in 1925 took the material from to produce his *Camellia x williamsii* hybrid" and with that parting comment he turned and slowly walked away. I looked at the camellia and then at Philip's retreating back and wondered if some day there might be a Philip Tregunna hybrid somewhere in the grounds.

It was a long while before I was able to fully take in that first visit, I kept going over different parts of the day in my mind. Were they really that tall, was the colour really that intense, was the fragrance really that strong? I've since been back several times just to confirm and I'm delighted to say that Caerhays has never let me down, even to the extent that there is now a magnolia in the grounds called Philip Tregunna.

Opposite 95. A fine example of *Michelia doltsopa*

68

96. *Pieris* 'Forest Flame' with primroses

98. Delightful walkway with magnolias, rhododendrons and camellias all on the Main Ride

99. Spring carpet of primroses

100. Kaleidoscope of spring colours

101. Magnolia on the Main Ride

103. *Magnolia* 'Caerhays Surprise'

102. Proud Peacock

104. *Camellia* 'Dream Castle'

105. *Michelia doltsopa* flowers

106. *Camellia* 'Galaxie'

107. Spring selection of primulas and cyclamen

108. *Pieris* 'Forest Flame'

109. Spring selection of primulas

Trewithen

Trewithen

Just after the idea of a book on the great gardens of Cornwall was first discussed, I happened to meet up with a quite famous gardener, one that, over the years had regularly inspired me, through his television programmes, to visit scores of gardens around the country. "Well, if it's Cornwall", he said," then the first on your list has got to be Trewithen!" He went on to extol the virtues of Trewithen's plant collection, and landscape. Our conversation passed onto other things and it was only, as he was getting back into his car, that he returned to the subject. "Now remember to include Trewithen, it has an excellent reputation", and with that he was gone.

Trewithen certainly was on our list and he was right, it did have a good reputation, but reputations can be hard to live up to and sadly, at times, reflect a glorious past rather than, the more accurate tired or tarnished present. This was reflected in our Cornish gardens list, a couple of quite famous gardens had already, following our visits, been scored off. So it was with a certain amount of trepidation that on a late spring afternoon I turned off the St Austell to Truro road and followed the signs to Trewithen.

Soon I found myself travelling through glorious parkland with ancient oaks, sycamores and beech on either side. It felt like old England, there was nothing in the landscape to jar the eye, this part of the estate could have changed little in the last two hundred years. I passed a small lake on my right, surrounded by a cluster of farm buildings, then to the left, a stable block and clock tower, beyond which stood a handsome, slate roofed, grey granite house. On the lawn in front of the house the Union flag was fluttering in the breeze.

I pulled into the garden car park, which lay a hundred yards or so beyond the house, bought a cup of tea and settled down on a picnic bench with my guide map. Time to plan the route ahead; I'll make for the Walled Garden first of all, then the Main Lawn, along Camellia Walk and down into the Wild Garden. Route planning is something I habitually do before every garden visit, although I have never managed to stick to a route yet. That doesn't matter, it's the planning that I enjoy, seeing what is on offer and anticipating the delights to come. Besides a good garden should encourage one to stray from the well-trodden path.

Not wishing to delay a moment longer I make my way through a plant centre brimming with unusual trees and shrubs and on into the garden. "Mind the guy ropes", says the lady at the gate. Seeing my puzzled expression, she explains that a large marquee has been erected on the Main Lawn, in readiness for a charity function, organised by the present owner of Trewithen, Michael Galsworthy, it is to be attended by Her Royal Highness, The Princess Royal.

Just a few yards inside the gate and my spirit soars, a wonderful *Cornus controversa* 'Variegata' commands attention, not only for its striking silver and green foliage but also its profusion of creamy-white flowers. There is a delightful sweet fragrance in the air, but it is not coming from the Cornus. Following the path outside the walled garden, my first detour of the day leads me towards a group of evergreen trees with superb, rusty-red flaking bark, as I get closer, so the fragrance gets stronger. They are myrtles, *Myrtus luma* and *lechleriana*, in some cases up to twenty feet tall. *Myrtus lechleriana*, is smothered in frothy white flower, from which emits this heavenly scent. Alongside, contrasting so well with the white myrtle flowers, is *Pieris formosa* var *forrestii*, with brilliant red young foliage. Now, we have all seen the *Pieris formosa* hybrid, 'Forest Flame', it is a favourite with gardeners throughout the country, but how many of us have seen the parent growing in the wild, very few I would suggest, me included. So come to Trewithen and see the next best thing, a whole forest of pieris, with great tree trunks up to one foot across. You will be able to walk beneath them, in virtual darkness, so dense is the evergreen canopy overhead. Close by is another plant from Formosa, (Taiwan), *Acer rubescens*. This beautiful maple is very rare, not only in the wild but also within cultivation. It has attractive striped bark and a red leaf-stalk. Perhaps not the most flamboyant of plants on display at Trewithen, nevertheless, because of its rarity, its a real gem and one not to be missed.

By now, I have of course missed the entrance to the Walled Garden, but before I have a chance to re-trace my steps, I catch sight of one of my favourite flowering trees, *Davidia involucrata*, the Pocket Handkerchief Tree, growing in between the Walled Garden and the house. What a marvellous display of flowers too, it is covered from head to foot with hanging white bracts. On closer inspection I can see that sometime in the past it has suffered from die-back and so has been pollarded, that is cut back hard and allowed to re-grow. The re-growth has been excellent, the tree looking good for at least another fifty years. Beyond, I can see the start of the Main Lawn and some brilliant flashes of colour, flame orange and gold, from great banks of deciduous azaleas. It would be very easy to head off in their direction, deeper into the garden. In the short time I had been at Trewithen, I had managed to get

Previous pages 110. Colourful panorama of Rhododendrons and Azaleas a feel for the kind of garden I was exploring and it was exciting to say the least. It was an informal garden, with winding, grey gravel paths, that curved out of view, behind spectacular flowering shrubs or ornamental trees in the distance. One never saw it all, there was always something more, something special, enticing one to follow on to the next bend and then the next. It was a clever way of drawing the visitor around the garden and it worked. However, I was determined to make one last attempt to enter the Walled Garden, so turning my back on the delights that lay ahead, I retraced my steps until I came to a gateway in the high red brick wall.

In marked contrast to the rest of the garden, the Walled Garden is quite formal by design, with rectangular beds and symmetrical pathways. It is also much older, having been constructed, along with the house in the eighteenth century. It was actually built as a herb garden, but by the beginning of the twentieth century it was being used as a drying ground, by the laundry maids doing the weekly washing for the house. Today, things are quite different, the garden is awash with botanical colour. There are plants in flower here from all over the world. On entering, a magnificent *Wisteria sinensis* hangs down from an old pergola. It has a wonderful old, craggy, gnarled trunk, that looks like it has been around since the laundry days. Growing against the walls is the tender *Clianthus puniceus*, the Lobster's Claw from New Zealand. Its bright red flowers combining so well with the fleshy, dark green leaves of a neighbouring fig, *Ficus carica*. An evergreen, sweetly scented clematis, *Clematis armandii*, grows vigorously, obviously enjoying the warmth of this sheltered garden. However, pride of place has to go to a plant that originated at Trewithen, *Ceanothus arboreus* 'Trewithen Blue', the Californian Lilac. It has the deepest, electric blue flowers imaginable. Two stone eagles look down from the terrace, almost daring anyone to speak in this tranquil place. There is a great peace here, the only sound coming from a little fountain trickling into a shallow, rectangular pond at the other end of the garden. Two delightful bronze otters stare cautiously at anyone approaching the pond, or are they just keeping an eye on the eagles? Peering into the garden, from the other side of the brick wall, is a *Liquidambar styraciflua* and here and there the bright red foliage of *Pieris fomosa* var *forrestii*, can just be seen. Later in the year, the garden will be full of fragrance from dozens of roses, growing in neatly edged beds, bordered by granite setts that came from the Redruth tramway in 1910.

I could linger in the Walled Garden for the rest of the afternoon, but voices from the other side of the wall remind me there is still much to be seen. Leaving by the doorway nearest the house, I walk along the terrace until I reach the Main Lawn. Here in front of me is a linear meandering glade, stretching southwards for some two hundred yards. At least there should be, but today well, let's say one hundred yards of it is under canvas. It is the great marquee for tonight's charity event. The interesting thing is, rather than the marquee dominating the lawn, the borders either side of the lawn dominate the marquee. If anything, it makes the glade look larger than it actually is.

The glade really is a remarkable feat of garden landscaping, one that has become a model for many other glades throughout Britain. It was created by George Johnstone, soon after the First World War. George Johnstone had inherited the Trewithen estate from his father in 1904. Trewithen is Cornish for 'the house in the spinney' and in 1904 that is exactly what it was. During the eighteenth century, George Johnstone's ancestors had carried out extensive tree planting throughout the estate, virtually creating a forest right up to the doors of the house. In George Johnstone's own words, "it was necessary to take an axe and claim air and light from amongst the trees, first for the house and those that should live in it, and then for the plants that must share the fortunes of the owner". This done, he began to introduce hundreds of exotic plants, particularly rhododendrons, into the glades created by the fellings. During the first world war, three hundred beech trees were felled by government order for the war effort, the bulk of them from the plantations directly behind the house. This provided the space necessary for George Johnstone to mark out and plan his great glade.

You will have heard of, 'around the world in eighty days', well without leaving the four borders of the Main Lawn, it is possible to circumnavigate the globe in about eighty minutes, that's taking into account the odd entanglement with guy ropes along the way. The only question I had to answer, as I stood on the terrace to the house, was where do I start first. Adjacent to the lawn itself, are the lower growing flowering shrubs, wave upon wave of rhododendrons, azaleas, camellias, corylopsis, viburnums and berberis. The colour combinations are absolutely magnificent, in places breaching the lawn edge with a flood of red, yellow and white.

Behind, are the larger, tree rhododendrons, enkianthus, embothrium, Japanese Acers and the smaller magnolias. Finally the upper canopy, the crowning glory, with further species of magnolias, *Betula*, *Nothofagus* and yet more magnolias. The overall picture is stunning, I can think of no garden that combines these plants to greater effect. There are so many individual plants that I could mention, but I would be in danger of creating a comparable volume to, 'The Hillier manual of Trees and Shrubs', so I shall stick with just a few that stopped me in my tracks. Great burgundy mounds of *Berberis thunbergii*, 'Rose Glow', wonderful fragrant, drooping white flower heads of *Magnolia wilsonii*, *Enkianthus campanulatus* dripping with sweetly scented, bell-shaped flowers, loved by bees. *Rehderodendron macrocarpum*, with exquisite styrax-like flowers, thirty feet tall *Embothrium coccineum*, the Chilean Fire Bush, every branch a mass of burning embers. At sixty feet tall *Magnolia campbellii* var. *mollicomata*, the tallest in Britain, *Stuartia sinensis*, with wonderful wrinkled bark just like an elephants leg, again the tallest of its kind in Britain. The shaggy, buff-pink bark of *Betula maximowicziana*. Monarch Birch from Japan, again another champion tree. I could carry on, but words alone cannot do justice to this astounding collection. All I can say is, if you are planning to visit Cornish gardens in the near future make sure this is one of them.

Completely overwhelmed, I leave the glade through the Alison Johnstone bay, named in honour of the wife of George Johnstone. On the way I pass a superb group of *Viburnum betulifolium*, still holding on to last year's bright red fruits in combination with this year's white flowers. Every few steps I gaze in awe at another botanical jewel, such as *Nothofagus menziesii*, the Silver Beech, from New Zealand and close by an enormous *Nothofagus nervosa* from Chile. One of the problems with being a 'tree gazer', the equivalent to the 'twitcher' in the bird world, is a propensity for a stiff neck. So, guide map in hand I decide it is time to get back on route for the Wild Garden, passing along Camellia Walk on the way. Along the southern and south-western edges to the gardens are signs of the tremendous gales of January 1990. A lot of the mature beeches and sycamore overstory has been lost. Replanting has taken place with, in particular, *Pinus radiata* the Monterey Pine, which is growing well, even so, it will be well into the next century before an effective wind-break is re-established.

The Camellia Walk is a winding gravel path, bordered on both sides by glossy evergreen leaves for most of the year. However in early spring, it bursts into life with a fantastic display of pink and white blooms. There are hundreds of camellias in this area, including specialities developed at Trewithen, such as, 'Trewithen Pink', 'Elizabeth Johnstone' and 'Glenn's Orbit', which is a seedling of *Camellia* 'Donation', that first flowered, at Trewithen on the day that the American astronaut, Colonel Glenn completed the first earth orbit. To see the camellia displays at their best one needs to visit in March.

At the end of the Camellia Walk is a shady dell, known as the 'Cock Pit'. Putting aside the obvious connotations in the name, it is a delightful area, quite different in style to the rest of Trewithen. Damp stone steps take one down through moss covered rocks and exotic tree ferns, *Dicksonia antarctica*. Look out for the lovely, *Piptanthus nepalensis*, it has bright yellow laburnum-like flowers in May, which stand out in this shady spot like phosphorus. Just before I break cover and head out across the open grassy area known as Little Downs, I am stopped in my tracks by a stunning display of fragrant, mustard-yellow flowers against a backdrop of bright green evergreen leaves. It is another south American plant, *Azara lanceolata* and another to add to my list of choice plants for sheltered areas.

Trewithen really is a plantsman's paradise, crossing the downs, there are flowering trees in every direction including, *Aesculus indica*, the Indian Horse Chestnut and *Paulownia tomentosa*, the Foxglove Tree. Great drifts of bluebells lead into the Coronation Planting of 1937, with a lovely *Magnolia sprengeri* 'Diva', saving the last of its gigantic, shell-pink blooms for my visit. Beyond lies the Wild Garden, where candelabra primulas and skunk cabbage *Lysichiton americanus* clamour for supremacy alongside a pond created in an old quarry area. There is just so much to see at Trewithen it is difficult to know where to start and to finish. I am conscious that although I have completed the route I marked on my map, there are whole areas I have not touched. Perhaps on my next visit I can put this right.

As I make my way back towards the gate and car park beyond, guests are already beginning to arrive for the charity event in the marquee. I won't forget that marquee, more importantly I will not forget the plants. Already I have an image of Trewithen in my mind and I have hardly left the grounds. It is of shaded, gently curving paths, framed on both sides and from above by masses of pink, white and lilac flowers. I think I can go back and tell my television gardening friend that Trewithen, through the careful management of the garden by Michael Galsworthy and his staff, has maintained its excellent reputation and is still well and truly on our list.

Opposite 111. The Main Lawn to the house

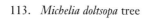
113. *Michelia doltsopa* tree

112. *Michelia doltsopa* flowers

114. Spring flowers in The Cockpit

115. *Hydrangea paniculata*

116. *Rhododendron* 'Cornish Red' on the Main Lawn

118. Inside the walled garden

117. Pieris and Azaleas

119. *Camellia* 'Joan Trehane'

120. *Rhododendron* 'Goldsworth Yellow'

121. *Camellia* 'Debbie'

122. *Clianthus puniceus*

123. *Ceanothus arboreus* 'Trewithen Blue'

124. Skunk Cabbage *Lysichiton americanus*

Chyverton

Chyverton

There is an old saying which goes something like, "know the garden, know the gardener", and nowhere can this be more appropriate than at Chyverton, the home of Nigel Holman. Nigel is owner, head gardener, official guide, chief mechanic and just about anything else you might like to mention. When I met him for the first time, his sleeves were rolled up to his armpits, he had a greasy spanner in a greasy hand and he was trying to breathe life back into a ride-on lawn mower, that really should have been put out to grass years before.

I think I was the excuse he had been looking for and within two minutes the abandoned red lifeless machine was just a faint dot in the middle of a rolling Georgian landscape as we walked towards the woodland. Nigel had found a better use for his spanner, it made an admirable 'pointer', which he began to frantically wave in the direction of his 'babies'. Nigel Holman, 'came out' long before it became fashionable under Royal patronage. "I freely admit to talking to my magnolias", he said in a magazine article in the 1980's. Well, whatever he did, and still does, seems to have worked, plants grow for him in a way that they never will for anyone else.

Chyverton is different, it is not like any other Cornish garden, in fact it is not like any other garden at all. The landscape is different, the plants are different (some of them), the style of gardening is different and the gardener is, well the gardener is Nigel Holman, son of Treve Holman, plantsman 'extraordinaire'.

Let's start with the landscape, most of the great Cornish gardens are situated close to the sea. Normally in a sheltered valley or south facing combe, they have lots of facilities for visitors and quite often lots of visitors, Chyverton has neither. Chyverton is in the centre of the peninsula, not far from the famous wind turbine site at Newlyn Down. Why did they put the turbines there ... because it is one of the most exposed sites in Cornwall. Chyverton gains its shelter from mature woodland, mostly oak, ash, beech and sycamore that surrounds the twenty acre garden. The garden is in essence a Georgian landscape, that has incorporated exotic plants from such locations as the Himalayas, China and Japan as they became available. It is not a garden created specifically to house them. So, at Chyverton you will find a vast expanse of grass, sweeping down to a lake and a graceful, arching, brick built bridge leading to woodland on the other side.

The original garden was designed by John Thomas, who lived at Chyverton from 1770 to 1825. It was he who planted up many of the woodlands surrounding the garden. Rhododendrons, of which there are many, started to arrive during the late 1800's and early 1900's, under the ownership of John Thomas-Peter. One plant that Chyverton does have in common with other Cornish gardens is *Rhododendron* 'Cornish Red', there is a magnificent specimen alongside the lake, close to the bridge. 'Alongside', is probably the wrong word, in the lake would be a more appropriate description. In May, great trusses of pinkish-red blooms drip down into the water, indeed it is hard to tell where plant ends and reflection begins. As the petals fall so the lake acquires a red shoreline as the petals drift against the banks. *Rhododendron* 'Cornish Red' is a hybrid between *Rhododendron Catawbiense* from North America and *Rhododendron arboreum*, from the Himalayas, and every Cornish garden seems to have at least one.

In 1924, the estate was purchased by Treve Holman, and that is when the introduction of new species to the garden really took off. Both J. C. Williams of Caerhays Castle and George Johnstone of Trewithen provided plants and in 1929 Harold Hillier visited. Seed also arrived at Chyverton from some of Frank Kingdon-Ward's plant hunting expeditions to China in the 1930's. In 1959 Treve Holman died and Nigel took on the job of maintaining and expanding the collection. He is still there today, as enthusiastic and pioneering as any of his predecessors.

I had telephoned Nigel the week before my visit, to let him know I was coming and to check what would be a suitable time for him. The gardens are open to the public, but by appointment only. "Anytime dear boy", had been his reply, so we arranged for early afternoon. On the map it looked simple, along the A30 and turn off at Zelah. Well, yes it is, but be ready for the turning, because if you miss it you are on your way to Redruth! The fun is not over even when you are on the right road, for the entrance to the garden has limited signing and gives no indication of what lays behind the hedgerows and shelter belts. Once inside a shaded track descends steeply, past farm buildings and without warning ends in a turning area directly in front of the house. On the left, a wonderful old *Wisteria sinensis* rambles and shambles along a hoop iron, railing fence. In late spring the combination of its long deep lilac flowers, with pink and red rhododendron blooms emerging from uncut herbage is quite remarkable. It is a stunning start to a magical tour and a taste of things to come.

Spanner still in hand, Nigel leads me to a plant just up the hill from

Previous pages 125. Treve Holman Memorial Bridge

the house with lush, tropical looking leaves some two feet long. Apparently the leaves are still expanding, by the time summer arrives they will be close on three feet. It is *Magnolia macrophylla dealbata*, a Mexican species, which was planted in 1988. Although there were some doubts about its hardiness, the young plant flowered three years later, it was the first flowering in Europe for this particular species. "What's your secret of success", I ask. "Plant them well and then do nothing", he says almost defiantly, "other than the occasional chat of course. No chemicals, just mulch, but be aware preparation is everything". His father used to say, one shilling for the plant, one pound for the hole.

Then we are off at a breath-taking rate, spinning through the border that is top side to the lawn pausing only to look at a *Ginkgo biloba*, planted by his father in 1930. Our next stop is a recently introduced conifer, *Pinus bhutanica*, Bhutan Pine, comparatively rare in its native habitat and introduced to Chyverton via the Conifer Conservation Programme created at the Royal Botanic Garden in Edinburgh. Then one of the most delightful rhododendrons of all, *Rhododendron quinquefolium*, a deciduous rhododendron with diamond-shaped leaves, lime green with a pink border, and the most exquisite flower imaginable, small bell-shaped, pure white with green spots. On the eastern end of the house we pass before *Magnolia wilsonii*, flowering like mad, then it's off across the lawn into the grounds below the house, passing on the way the most magnificent prostrate oak. This giant fallen veteran has limbs the size of tree trunks and the trunk itself, when standing, would have taken half a dozen people, arms outstretched, to circumnavigate. It is probably some three hundred years old, which means it would have looked down upon John Thomas, purposefully striding this wooded valley, on the way to creating his Georgian landscape.

Chyverton is neither formal nor prissy and that is part of its attraction. It is gardening at the sharp end, there are no hoards of gardeners ensuring every path is manicured. At times there is no path at all, just a beaten track, as on the inside of a wonderful hedge of *Myrtus luma*, running down the western edge of the lawn, from the house to the water. Planted in 1948 it is now over twenty feet tall and what a sight, with its cinnamon coloured bark and dark evergreen foliage. Where the myrtle hedge ends so the magnolias begin, giant, cabbage-like pink flowers on *Magnolia campbellii* in March, *Magnolia x soulangeana* pink goblets in April and cream-coloured heavily scented flowers of *Magnolia hypoluca* in May and June, in all there are over twenty different magnolias within the grounds. Deep in the valley by a shady rectangular pool is a superb specimen of *Viburnum plicatum* 'Mariesii', its white regularly layered flowers giving the plant the effect of a snow laden bush. On the far side of the pool Nigel proudly points out to me a mature *Dacrydium franklinii*, the rare Huon Pine from Tasmania with slender drooping branches.

Moving away from the water's edge we venture into the woodland to the north of the lake. In here, beneath dappled shade is a whole group of Japanese maples, including *Acer palmatum* 'Atropurpureum', planted in 1932 to create autumn colour that would be visible from the house. It worked, but by now that seems of no surprise for it all seems to work. The place is really quite magical, tiny seedlings of tender plants are planted in the woodland and just left and they grow, because, it seems, that is what Nigel Holman expects them to do.

Nigel has recently realised an ambition which will shortly mean, seedlings he plants at Chyverton will have actually been collected as seed by him in the wild, rather than arriving via some anonymous donor. In October 1996 Nigel joined a plant hunting expedition to China, bringing back many new species for the garden. "It was a dream come true" he says, "my only regret is that my father did not have the same opportunity".

Of course, some of these new species will struggle to survive but that's fine because whatever grows at Chyverton has to be able to fend for itself, it is the survival of the fittest.

There are all together twenty nine little sheltered glades, or rooms, tucked away in this woodland and Nigel leads me to them all in turn, pointing out the rarities in each. *Lomatia ferruginea*, *Drimys lanceolata*, *Enkianthus deflexus*, *Rhododendron pachytrichum* and a superb specimen of *Styrax japonica*, the Snowball Tree, which is believed to be one of the largest in Britain. It has exquisite hanging, bell-shaped white flowers, which in late spring completely cover the tree, giving an absolutely magical appearance. All the time alongside there are great flowering towers of colourful rhododendrons. Yes, it is a plantsman's garden and there will be those who will drool over many of the names mentioned here. Chyverton is however much more than that, you may have little horticultural knowledge but that will not stop you enjoying this garden, it has a spirit that gets under the skin. The long vistas across the lawn to the lake and the woodland beyond will delight, as will the intimate plantings around the house.

One of my favourite vistas at Chyverton is the view from the lakeside looking away from the bridge. Wonderful, rampant, lush vegetation crowds the water's edge, like cattle at a drinking hole, pushing and jostling for space. The shades of green in this area are quite amazing particularly when the sun catches the bank, ranging from the richest summer green of skunk cabbage, *Lysichiton americanus* to the dark sombre leaves of rhododendrons.

There is one other feature I have yet to mention and it was the last area that Nigel took me to. Downstream from the red brick bridge is a bog garden and it was here that I lost my heart to Chyverton. Once past the bridge the ribbon lake narrows to a stream, that tumbles down the valley to the east. The ground is boggy and contains a magnificent display of *Lysichiton americanus*, the yellow spotted Skunk Cabbage. Alongside grow ferns, orchids and candelabra primulas by the thousand. In late spring it is a garden of beauty beyond belief. At one point where the rhododendrons creep down to the water's edge there is a curving wooden bridge, reminiscent of Monet's Bridge in Giverny. This one is the Treve Holman Memorial Bridge. Out of the woodwork grow lichens like whiskers, covering the hand rails and supports in a greeny-grey down. Throughout the garden the same has happened to woodland seats, it looks like no one has sat on them for decades. They have become part of the garden and who would now dare to sit on them!

As we make our way back up to the house, Nigel notices the ride on mower, "Oh Lord", he says, "I do wish there was less grass, it does so hamper the gardening".

Opposite 126. Magnificent rhododendron by the lake with floating petals

127. Azaleas and bluebells by lichen covered seat

128. *Wisteria sinensis* by the house

129. Skunk Cabbage *Lysichiton americanus* in the stream

130. Lush greens by the lake in high summer

131. A fine *Rhododendron* 'Cornish Red' by the main lawn

132. The lakeside in early spring

133. *Viburnum plicatum* 'Mariesii' in the Woodland Garden

134. Bridge with stream full of *Lysichiton americanus*

135. *Rhododendron pachytrichum*

136. Evening sunshine by the Treve Holman Bridge

137. *Acer palmatum* 'Atropurpureum' amongst deciduous Azaleas

138. *Styrax japonica* flowers

139. A fine specimen of a *Styrax japonica* tree

141. Hybrid orchids by the bridge

140. Tree Rhododendron on the Main Drive

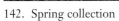

142. Spring collection

143. *Magnolia stellata*

144. Deciduous Azaleas with lichen covered seat

145. *Lysichiton camtschatcensis*

146. *Rhododendron pachytrichum*

147. Rose Betty Sherriff

Trelissick

Trelissick

Even if one of the most beautiful gardens in Cornwall wasn't situated just beyond the eastern fringes of this well laid out car park, I guarantee that parking space would still be at a premium. For at Trelissick just the approach is enough to set my pulse racing. It is the only car park to a garden, that I can think of, that is a destination in its own right. Without leaving the car, one can enjoy the most stunning coastal scenery imaginable. A glorious panoramic view down the Carrick Roads, a deep navigable channel of water which meanders from Trelissick towards Falmouth Bay and the open sea beyond. Water is never far away during a visit to Trelissick, the estate sits high up in the middle of a wooded peninsula, with Lamouth Creek to the north, the River Fal to the east and the Carrick Roads and Channals Creek to the south and west. Even when immersed within the lush vegetation of the gardens, one is still likely to catch a glimpse of open water or hear the comings and goings of the King Harry Ferry, some one hundred and fifty feet below.

The setting for Trelissick is quite remarkable and so it is no wonder that as long ago as the eighteenth century, this delightful wooded peninsula already boasted a country house estate, complete with a three hundred and fifty acre landscaped park. Captain John Lawrence of the Cornish militia built the original house in 1750. It was a plain two-storey villa with a recessed verandah on the southern front, facing Falmouth Bay. On Captain Lawrence's death in 1800, the estate was sold to Ralph Allen Daniell whose family fortune had been made in the Cornish tin and copper mining industries. Daniell laid out miles of carriage rides through the park, many of which are still in existence today, and set about planting new woodlands around the estate and a kitchen garden beside the house. In 1832, Daniell sold Trelissick to the Earl of Falmouth, whose great house across the River Fal at Tregothnan can still be seen, from a curved wooden seat and viewpoint within Trelissick garden itself. Lord Falmouth held Trelissick for little more than twelve years before selling to John Davies Gilbert in 1844.

It was his son, Carew Davies Gilbert, who set about creating much of the landscape so admired and loved by those who visit Trelissick today. Gilbert planted a matrix of woodland shelter belts to protect the garden from the ferocious storms which frequently sweep in from the Atlantic. He then began to introduce into the garden many exotic tress and shrubs from his extensive travels in North and South America, Japan and southern Europe, including probably one of Trelissick's finest

trees, a superb Japanese Cedar, *Cryptomeria japonica*. Planted in 1898, this magnificent specimen can still be seen, with its great sweeping branches polished smooth following endless caressing by admiring hands over the years. It is the central feature of the Main Lawn, just beyond the kitchen garden and hopefully will continue to be so, well into the next century. The Gilberts held the estate until 1920, when it was sold to Leonard Daneham Cunliffe, Governor of the Bank of England. His step daughter, Ida Copeland inherited the estate in 1937.

Over the next twenty years Mrs Copeland, along with her husband Ronald, transformed the garden, planting numerous spring flowering cherries, camellias and rhododendrons, including many hybrid rhododendrons from Bodnant Gardens in North Wales. They also began to convert an old orchard, known as Carcaddon, north of the road to the King Harry Ferry, into a marvellous collection of trees and shrubs from all corners of the temperate world, including many hydrangea species never previously grown at Trelissick. In 1955, Ida Copeland gave Trelissick House, three hundred and seventy six acres of park and woodland and twenty five acres of garden to the National Trust. The house remains the family home and is not regularly open to the public. The gardens thankfully are and they really are an absolute delight, at any time of year but particularly in spring, when the whole area erupts with fragrant blossom. I love it and cannot get enough of it. If I happen to miss my regular April visit to Trelissick, then somehow I feel I just haven't seen the best that spring has to offer.

Trelissick is not a wild Cornish garden, where rampaging 'Cornish Red' rhododendrons smother all but the most stalwart shade bearers and seedling tree ferns spring like watercress from damp, rich acid soils. Trelissick has manicured lawns, neatly edged beds and well maintained paths, particularly in the areas nearest the house and garden entrance. Here virtually in the shade of a stone conical water tower, resplendent with squirrel weathervane, one finds a whole host of intimate walled gardens and south facing nooks and crannies. The warmest of these must be the little Parsley Garden, tucked into the angle of two, red bricked, garden walls. Originally used for growing early vegetables, flowers and herbs for the house, it now contains, amongst the parsley, an assortment of tender plants including *Azara integrifolia*, *Clematis rehderiana* and a lovely *Cestrum aurantiacum*, with bright orange and red trumpet-shaped flowers, soaking up the warmth from the soft, sun baked walls. Opposite the Parsley Garden, beyond a wall lost beneath prolific fragrant blooms of *Rosa chinensis* "Mutabilis' lies the Fig Garden.

Previous pages 146. Cherry Blossom in Carcaddon

Here, twenty year old 'Brown Turkey' fig cultivars, push and jostle for space in a tiny triangular garden, backed by a collection of variegated ivies growing up the wall of an adjoining stable block. Take a moment or two off from your tour of the garden to view the quite unique collection of equestrian memorabilia inside the stable block. I am the first to admit, my knowledge of the horse world is limited, but even I find this collection fascinating and alongside is a smaller exhibition devoted to the Trelissick Estate.

If however, like me, it is the plants that really stir your blood, you will soon find yourself heading for the herbaceous borders surrounding the old kitchen garden. Deliberately planted for all season pleasure, they are brimming with exciting plants many rarely seen outdoors east of the Tamar. In summer *Magnolia grandiflora* 'Gallissonnière' proudly displays wonderfully scented, creamy white flowers, some eight to ten inches across, alongside purple drifts of *Liatris spicata*, 'Gay feathers', punctured here and there by handsome, long mid-green leaves and showy orange coloured flower spikes of *Cautleya spicata*. Pink, red and Cambridge blue, mophead hydrangeas, flower on well into autumn creating splashes of colour beneath a magical selection of Japanese Maple cultivars of *Acer palmatum* and *japonicum*, blushing like beacons in October and early November.

It is for spring however that the borders throughout Trelissick reserve their greatest show. Carpets of *Primula*, including the delightful pink petalled *Primula* 'Garryarde Guinevere', run beneath a breathtaking assortment of spring flowering shrubs. Deep violet flowers of *Abutilon x suntense* 'Jermyns', mix with deliciously scented *Viburnum x burkwoodii* and the fragrant star shaped white flowers of *Drimys winteri*, Winters Bark. Where the borders edge the Main Lawn, a superb *Azara serrata*, with brilliant yellow flowers literally covering the whole plant, seems to hover like a hazy yellow cloud, beneath a large *Ailanthus altissima*, Tree Of Heaven. Close by, the soft, feathery evergreen foliage of *Chamaecyparis pisifera* 'Filifera' provides the perfect contrast for rich, chestnut-red stems of *Myrtus luma*. The borders are deep and in places fragmented by great brick arched supports for the leaning kitchen garden wall, held up also it seems, by large tree rhododendrons, *Rhododendron arboreum* and *Rhododendron* 'Cornish Red', which beckon like sirens, the casual visitor, to explore further into the garden, towards the woodland walks which lie beyond the Main Lawn.

From here the eye is carried across the valley to the many specimen trees on the slopes of Carcaddon. To get there, one has to cross the busy, sunken road which bisects the garden and leads on down to the quayside on the River Fal, where one can board the King Harry Ferry for the five minute crossing to St. Mawes. The link to Carcaddon is a delightful wooden bridge, surmounted by carved wooden pine cones. Although a recent replacement for a much older brick structure, this rustic bridge looks like it has been there since Gilberts day and once across, the whole of Carcaddon opens out before one. 'Car' or 'Caer' indicates a fortified place or castle, the only structure present today is a rustic thatched summerhouse, its design reflected in that of the bridge. For me it acts like a magnet, insisting I spend a few minutes sitting quietly within its shady recess, watching pheasants wander through great banks of newly planted hydrangeas, before heading out to start my plant exploration of Carcaddon. Inside the summerhouse, the walls and ceiling contain patterns, cleverly created using *Pinus radiata*, Monterey Pine cones. This rustic retreat offers probably one of the finest views of these magnificent gardens and one that immediately comes to mind whenever Trelissick is mentioned.

Although the conversion of Carcaddon from orchard to garden began just before the Second World War and was hastened by the National Trust in the 1960's, there are still a number of stunning examples of earlier tree plantings, including a gnarled old pollard oak in the lawn close to the summerhouse and a group of weather beaten *Cupressus macrocarpa* to the western end. Two of the finest ornamental trees of all are two Japanese cherries, *Prunus* 'Tai Haku' and *Prunus* 'Kanzan', they stand side by side, no more than fifteen feet apart, with their branches entwined. In spring their respective white and deep pink blossom intermingle to delightful effect, it is truly a sight not to be missed. Across the lawns splendid displays of *Narcissi* dance excitedly around scores of recently planted hybrid rhododendrons and hydrangeas. There are so many interesting plants throughout Carcaddon that it is difficult to pick out just a few to mention, but for me one of the finest spring flowering shrubs is a large broom, *Cytisus* 'Porlock' near the old pollard oak. When in flower it positively gleams and is visible from just about every part of the garden. To the western end of Carcaddon, close to the water tower, things have gone full circle, for here a recently planted orchard has been established containing Cornish apple varieties. In time it is hoped that this orchard will contain the definitive collection of Cornish apples, including varieties that would have been grown at Trelissick one hundred and fifty years ago.

Heading back across the rustic bridge, just a few steps to the left, leads one down into The Dell. Almost every Cornish garden worth its salt has one, some are grand beyond belief, the whole garden being created around combes which plunge headlong down into some salty estuary or other. Trelissick is no different, except this dell has a more genteel, almost refined feel about it, giving nothing away until one is deep within its grasp and totally committed. Here one finds, sheltered by dense, weeping, coniferous foliage, wonderful lush clumps of *Polygonatum x hybridum*, Solomon's Seal, covered in late spring with delightful clusters of greenish-white, tubular flowers. Mature specimens of *Dicksonia antarctica*, the Soft tree fern and *Trachycarpus fortunei*, the Chusan Palm abound, providing a real sense of exotica and great clumps of bamboo rule supreme, except of course for the rhododendrons and azaleas. Oh, the wonderful rhododendrons, their flowers fall about one like an avalanche, from the creamy-white *Rhododendron johnstoneanum* to the flaming red *Rhododendron thomsonii* and on to the brilliant yellow *Rhododendron* 'Mary Swaythling'. In spring the colours are so intense, every now and then one needs to focus beyond The Dell, just to reduce the risk of being completely overwhelmed. The views out from The Dell are truly memorable, across the valley to the white-washed walls of Ferris's Cottage, or eastwards to the River Fal and the ocean-going ships that anchor in its deep waters, just a stone's throw from the tree clad banks. In May the scent from scores of deciduous azaleas fills the air, adding to the feeling of intoxication, their fragrance settling in the bottom of The Dell, where a small runnel keeps moist an acidic bog garden. Here, gigantic rhubarb-like leaves of *Gunnera manicata* shelter a multitude of moisture loving plants, such as rodgersias, candelabra primulas, hostas and astilbes. Clambering out from The Dell is a breathtakingly beautiful *Azara serrata*, for once a plant outshining the showy performance of neighbouring rhododendrons, including a purple flowered *Rhododendron augustinii* and *Rhododendron* 'Gwillt King', a cultivar specially created at Trelissick. Higher up the slope, shrubs give way to grassy banks planted with spring flowering bulbs, mainly *Narcissi* and in particular, two named after members of the Copeland family, 'Irene' and 'Mary Copeland'.

Once the shoulder of The Dell is attained the path levels out and heads towards the river. Here, extensive plantings of blue and white hydrangeas grow happily beneath choice trees such as *Halesia carolina*, the Snowdrop Tree and a whole host of flowering cherries. The walk alongside the River Fal to the new summerhouse, built in 1996 to honour Jack Lilly, Head Gardener at Trelissick for many years, is delightful at any time of year, but ensure you walk beyond, to the Celtic Cross. Here the views across the river some one hundred and fifty feet below are stunning. It is said that at one time from this point, the local priest would preach to the fishermen in their boats far below before they set sail, the acoustics being especially good. True? … Who knows, nevertheless an intriguing story and I can confirm that voices do carry well in this area. I have often stood on this spot listening to conversations between passengers on the King Harry Ferry as it made its way across to the Roseland Peninsular. From here the path leads round to the west, passing a group of *Photina x fraseri* 'Red Robin' surrounding a young *Araucaria araucana*, the Chile Pine and suddenly almost without warning, the sparkling blue waters of the Carrick Roads and Falmouth Bay beyond come into view. Beneath two mighty *Quercus cerris*, Turkey Oaks, is positioned the original Victorian, Trelissick summerhouse, at one time overlooking the site of old tennis courts. These are now long gone, but the view to the sea has not changed, here is a place to linger and soak up not only the beauty of this marvellous garden but also the landscape beyond. Across the parkland one can just get a glimpse of the white pillared front to Trelissick House.

As the waning sun dips towards Channals Creek, ancient parkland oaks and beech begin to cast long shadows which creep slowly across the close cropped grass. Overhead, in the canopy of a group of old *Quercus ilex*, Holm Oak, part of the original shelter system planted by Carew Davies Gilbert more than one hundred and fifty years ago, a solitary rook calls across The Dell. This echoing call reminds me of a five minute warning bell, as if giving notice of the garden's imminent closure. Within seconds the whole rookery is alive, as each resident bird tries hard to call louder than its neighbour, ensuring that even the most hard of hearing visitor can have no excuse for lingering. I have to admit it is getting late and I should be leaving, reluctantly I head back towards the Main Lawn, passing beneath the leafy bowers of the Shaded Walk. It has been a wonderful day, once again Trelissick has turned on the magic. I know I have not seen all that this garden has to offer, perhaps I never will.

One thing is certain, I will be back, after all what would spring be without a visit to Trelissick?

Opposite 149. A full border of the Main Lawn

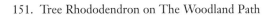
151. Tree Rhododendron on The Woodland Path

150. 'The Water Tower'

152. Rhododendrons and bluebells near The Dell

153. Red Hydrangeas near The Old Kitchen Garden

154. *Liatris spicata*

155. *Acer palmatum* in the Main Lawn border

156. Colourful border by The Old Kitchen Garden

157. *Cupressus macrocarpa* in Carcaddon

158. Alstroemeria, Gypsophila, Agapanthus in colourful border

159. Bridge from Carcaddon

160. View across The Dell to Ferris's Cottage

161. *Prunus* 'Kanzan' and 'Tai Haku' in Carcaddon

162. View to the River Fal through spring blossom and daffodils

163. Colourful border by The Old Kitchen Garden
including Verbena, Tradescantia, Canna and Liatris

164. Colourful collection of Hydrangeas at the
entrance of Carcaddon

165. Pink Gypsophila with Hydrangeas by Main Lawn

166. *Azara serrata*

167. *Cautleya spicata*

168. Astilbes in The Dell

Glendurgan

Glendurgan

There are some days you just know are going to be special, and from the moment I opened my eyes this morning, to a sun filled room and heard water lapping against the harbour wall, just yards from my window, I knew this was going to be one of them. I had spent the night in a small hotel right on the quayside at Mevagissey. For years I lived close to the sea, happy in the knowledge that during the summer I could leave my office at 5.00pm and be swimming in the sea half an hour later. It is now almost ten years since we moved to Gloucestershire, yet still I find it difficult to accept that the real coast is a couple of hours drive away. So to be able to combine my affection for the sea, with one of my other great pleasures in life, that is, wandering through other peoples gardens, is an absolute joy. Cornwall is of course best known for its coastline, but it is also famous for its gardens. The two are intrinsically linked, it is the sea which moderates the climate and allows Cornish gardeners the freedom to grow plants that in Gloucestershire gardeners can only dream of.

I had been working on the great gardens of Cornwall publication for quite some time, but today was the day I planned to return to one of my favourite Cornish gardens. A garden which can be entered straight from the coast and once within its luxuriant grounds, offers spectacular views of the sea from almost every quarter. Today was the day I was to return to Glendurgan.

Glendurgan is a collection of four verdant combes, or valleys, full of lush vegetation, flowing down to the banks of the Helford Estuary. The main valley runs almost due south. At one end sits Glendurgan House, at the other the delightful hamlet of Durgan, where a cluster of twenty or so white-washed cottages, formerly fishermen's cottages, huddle up close to the estuary. In between the house and the village is twenty five acres of glorious Cornish woodland garden.

The easiest approach to Glendurgan is from the Falmouth road. The garden itself being situated four miles or so south-west of Falmouth, close to the village of Mawnan Smith. Next door to Glendurgan sits Trebah, in places they almost rub shoulders. What is interesting is that although both gardens are in south facing combes, running down to the Helford River and both have a history of care by the same family, they couldn't be more different. Trebah is a close canopied, almost secretive valley, whereas Glendurgan holds nothing back, it opens itself to the visitor from the moment of arrival.

The first classic views of the sea appear, from the moment one arrives in the well maintained, gravelled car park. At a smart, National Trust entrance kiosk, complete with friendly staff, happy to inform you of the benefits of National Trust membership, one can obtain maps, guides and just about anything else. However, it is the plants I have come for, so a quick cup of coffee in the adjacent wooden chalet and then I'm off, rushing down the recently created curving path which leads to the Camellia Walk. Alongside the new path there are hundreds of young camellias, all planted in the last five years. There are traditional camellias here such as *Camellia japonica*, 'Pink Perfection', and the striking 'Lavinia Maggi', with pale pink and deep cerise stripes, however, the bulk are modern cultivars of *Camellia reticulata*. This plant is one of the most beautiful of all camellia species and has produced dozens of cultivars over the years. It was first introduced into Britain, from Western China, by the great Scottish plant collector, George Forrest, in 1924 and is perfectly hardy in most locations in Southern Britain. Some of the more modern cultivars of *Camellia reticulata* are however, slightly more tender than the parent, nevertheless they flourish in Gendurgan's benign, almost sub-tropical climate. Here you will find banks of beautiful pink and white blooms, from cultivars such as, 'Butterfly Wings', 'Crimson Rose' and 'Lion's Head'. Already, after just five years, they are combining to make a stunning entrance walk to the garden, that can only get even better as the years go by. At the end of the new path one turns right and enters the original Camellia Walk, planted by George Fox over one hundred years ago. These venerable, old specimens are in some cases over fifteen feet tall, arching together way above the path, to create a great tunnel of shiny, evergreen leaves and in spring, an enormous bower of blooms. Here you will find such lovely plants as 'Captain Rawes', 'Cornish Snow', Debutante', and the variegated leaves and dark red flowers of 'Ville de Nantes'. To see Glendurgan's camellia display at its best, you need to be here as early in the year as March or April. If you leave it much later then the peak will have passed and the ground will be covered with a soft layer of pink and white petals, which is in itself a sight to behold.

George Fox was the grandson of Alfred Fox, who purchased Glendurgan in 1823, having previously rented cellars and orchards at Durgan. The Fox family, from Falmouth, were one of the most influential and indeed wealthiest families, in the area. They were Quakers, as well as gardeners and had already acquired neighbouring Trebah and Penjerrick. They set about developing, on all of these

Previous pages 169. Bluebells and Tulip Tree *Liriodendron tulipifera* planted by Alfred Fox properties, some of the most beautiful gardens in Britain, creating, in their own words, "A small piece of Heaven on Earth". When Alfred purchased Glendurgan, it was mainly given over to fruit, there were several productive orchards throughout the estate. Along with his wife Sarah, they built a thatched cottage at the top of the valley, close to the present house and extended the orchards. They also began to plant great shelter belts of trees including lime, beech and ash, as well as *Quercus ilex*, Holm Oak and *Pinus radiata*, Monterey Pine. Once the trees were established, they began to turn the sheltered, stream-fed valleys into vast gardens, planting many exotic and ornamental trees and shrubs. Some plants were obtained readily from the family's other gardens, such as from Alfred's brother Charles, who was busy, at the same time, developing Trebah next door. Others came through the family's connections with the shipping industry. They managed to persuade a number of ship's captains to bring back new plant species from their travels abroad.

In 1833, Alfred planted, probably Glendurgan's most famous feature, a cherry laurel maze, alongside which he dug a pond and stocked it with trout. By the time George Fox took over Glendurgan in the 1890's, the bones of the garden were established. In addition to the Camellia Walk, George introduced many other species to the garden, in particular, spring flowering rhododendrons, which today produce some of the most spectacular displays of all. In 1962 the garden was given to the National Trust. The family still live at Glendurgan and have some involvement within the grounds, some one hundred and eighty years since Alfred Fox first arrived.

Leaving the shelter of the Camellia Walk, I emerge into bright sunshine and some of the most wonderful views imaginable. The path keeps to the head of the main valley, just below the house, and from here, on this late April morning, great billowing clouds of pink, red and white rhododendrons roll gracefully down the lush green valley sides to the estuary far below. It is as if, in this sheltered Cornish combe paradise has been created. The brilliance of the rhododendrons contrasts delightfully with the subtle, fresh greens from emerging foliage in the surrounding woodland. Open sweeps of wild flower meadowland drift in between the rhododendrons and the woodland edge. There are primroses, violets, bluebells, red campion and then, if that were not enough, thousands upon thousands of wild aquilegia. Their colours ranging from pure white, through every shade of blue possible, to the deepest purple. Was this what Alfred and Sarah Fox had in mind as they set about creating, "A small piece of Heaven on Earth?"

Above the path, in what is probably the warmest part of the garden, is a free-draining, south facing bank, interspersed with beds and borders leading up to a lawn in front of the house. On the shallow soils of this bank, sub-tropical plants such as *Agave americana*, the Century plant, from Mexico, thrive, throwing up from a rosette of sword-shaped, sharp toothed leaves, flower spikes up to twenty five feet tall. Do not hold your breath though, they can take fifty years or more to flower, (if you wait that long it most probably feels like a century). The ones here at Glendurgan are over forty years old, progeny from a plant that flowered and then died here in the 1950's. Adding to the tropical feel of this area, Chusan Palms, *Trachycarpus fortunei*, cast star-like shadows onto the bank. Whilst shrubs such as *Viburnum plicatum*, 'Mariesii', *Embothrium coccineum*, the Chilean Fire Bush and *Cornus kousa*, the Japanese Dogwood, add colour through their spectacular flower displays.

No matter where one walks at Glendurgan there are horticultural delights to drool over. Just beyond the Valley Head Path is the Holy Bank. A grassy bank, planted up with just about every tree that has an association with Christ. Grouping plants through their symbolic associations, is not a new idea, it was something the Victorians revelled in. Gathered together here are *Ailanthus altissima*, the Tree of Heaven, *Cercis siliquastrum*, the Judas Tree, *Paliurus-spina-christi*, Christ's Thorn, and a recent introduction, *Crataegus monogyna*, 'Biflora', the Glastonbury Thorn. From here it is an easy stroll, down the slope, beneath flowering magnolias and a magnificent multi-branched, *Thuja plicata*, Western Red Cedar to the Cherry Laurel Maze. It is said, Alfred Fox obtained his inspiration for the maze having visited the, then famous maze in the Sydney Gardens in Bath. The Glendurgan maze, has a route, in and out, of about three quarters of a mile. Its intricate design is viewed at its best, from the top of Manderson's Hill, on the east side of the valley. For the moment I want to explore the maze at close quarters. Following a period of decline, it underwent major restoration in 1992. All the laurel hedges were cut back to little more than waist high. Any gaps were enriched with young laurel clones, from the original plants. The paths were re-surfaced and a new, thatched summerhouse, a replica of the original from 1833, was erected in the centre. To look out, from the summerhouse, across the maze to the gardens beyond, on this warm, sunny, spring day is a privilege indeed. Surrounding the maze are trees and shrubs from all regions of the world, including a lovely specimen of *Paulownia tomentosa*, the Foxglove

Tree, from China. It has exquisite, purple-spikes of almost orchid-like flowers. Close by is the weeping form of the Katsura Tree, *Cercidiphyllum japonicum*, 'Pendulum', another great favourite of mine and one to look out for on an autumn visit to Glendurgan, when its leaves turn a clear butter yellow.

Beyond a giant clump of bamboo, just by the entrance to the maze, is the pond, its clear water alive with tadpoles. It is fed by a little runnel, which splashes down from the higher ground near the house. A rustic wooden bridge crosses to a small island, surrounded by ferns and surmounted by a lovely specimen of the Indian Cedar, *Cedrus deodara*. Slightly upstream from the pond, close to a thirty foot tall, *Rhododendron* 'Cornish Red', is a large, weeping, Swamp Cypress, *Taxodium distichum*, obviously loving the damp conditions of the stream side. It originates from the swampy ground of the Everglades region in Florida, where it produces strange, 'knee-like' growths from its roots, which appear in the water, quite some distance from the tree. Here at Glendurgan, these strange growths are beginning to develop in between the tree and the stream.

I could very easily linger in this area of the garden all day, discovering more and more unusual trees and shrubs, but I promised myself this morning, when I awoke in that sunny room in Mevagissey, that I would spend just a few minutes by the sea. So heading past two striking, Chinese Firs, *Cunninghamia lanceolata*, I make my way down through the lush vegetation of the Lower Valley, towards the hamlet of Durgan. The further I walk, the more dense and shaded the valley becomes and indeed more astounding in its content. *Dicksonia antarctica*, the Soft tree fern, is of course found in most Cornish gardens, but how about *Cyathea australis*, the Australian tree fern or *Musa basjoo*, the Banana Bush, or the low growing shrubby, *Cyathodes colensoi*, with its stiff, grey-green, evergreen foliage and pure white pitcher-like flowers. Glendurgan is a garden not to be under-estimated, there are botanical gems here found in few other gardens in Britain. Right in the middle of the Lower Valley, virtually covered by giant clumps of bamboo, is a wonderful bamboo bridge across the stream. No nails or screws were used in the construction, each bamboo pole being spliced to the next using sizel. In all some fifteen hundred feet of sizel rope was used during its construction, by National Trust staff in 1994 as a centenary project.

Continuing down alongside the stream, one passes an old cattle rush. A steep track bordered on either side by moss covered, dry stone walls, through which stock were brought to the stream to drink. Shortly afterwards a gate is reached and within minutes I am listening to water lapping on the sides of two yachts, moored just off the beach. Squinting in the bright sunshine reflecting off the water, I gaze across to the wooded fringes of the Lizard Peninsula. There are little coves and inlets all along this stretch of coast, smugglers country to be sure! Frenchman's Pill, (Frenchman's Creek in the Daphne du Maurier novel), is just upriver on the Lizard side.

With my nostrils still full of the salty sea air, I head back up a rough cobbled lane, to re-enter the garden, this time on the west side of the valley. Here, there are large groups of hydrangeas and rhododendrons, including *Rhododendron* 'Polar Bear'. One of the last rhododendrons to flower, this will still be doing its bit, with fragrant, pure white, trumpet-shaped flowers, when the hydrangeas start to flower in a couple of months time.

In the hot afternoon sunshine, I climb back up the steep winding pathways towards the Giant's Stride. An appropriate name for a series of rope swings, used by generations of children of the Fox family and now, as I approach, providing great fun for a family of visitors to the garden.

Now, what was it the lady in the National Trust kiosk said to me this morning, 'look out for the old giant by the cherry orchard'. Intrigued, I cross the valley just below the maze and make my way uphill, towards a cloud of white blossom in the distance. The path leads my weary legs, (there's a lot of ups and downs at Glendurgan), into a glade of cherries. Not the fruiting type, as would have been here in Alfred Fox's time, but flowering cherries, including stunning varieties such as *Prunus* 'Tai Haku', the Great White Cherry and *Prunus incisa* the Mount Fuji cherry. Beneath the cherries are carpets of bluebells, not yet faded by the sun, what a delightful spot this is. Now I'm here, I do not need to hunt out the old giant, in fact it looks like he is hunting me! A fantastic Tulip Tree, *Liriodendron tulipifera*, is just by the path in front of me. Boughs outstretched like giant arms, it seems to be trying to climb out of the ground. Well, I'm not going to stay around whilst he attempts it, besides its getting late and I have a long drive back to Gloucestershire ahead of me. I slowly make my way back up the path towards the car park, it has been a wonderful day, a really special day, but then I knew it always would be, any day is special at Glendurgan.

Opposite 170. View through the valley to the Helford Estuary

171. The pool with Astilbes and *Cedrus deodara*

172. Bamboo Bridge, a National Trust Centenary Project

173. Mature rhododendrons and azaleas in the valley

174. Upper Walk with rhododendrons and bluebells

175. *Prunus* 'Tai Haku' 'The Great White Cherry'

176. Valley view down to Swamp Cypress *Taxodium distichum*

177. Kurume Azalea

178. Camellia Walk with carpet of petals

179. Wild flowers in the valley

180. Primroses make their way through fallen petals

181. The new Maze of Cherry Laurel with the Thatched Summer House

182. The Lower Valley full of colourful rhododendrons

183. Japanese cherry blossom and bluebells

184. Valley view with Chusan Palms to the Helford Estuary

185. *Viburnum plucatum* with bluebells

186. Camellia Walk

187. Early purple orchids in the valley

Trebah

There are certain words which make me distinctively uneasy when used to describe a garden. Words like paradise, enchanting, uniquely beautiful, seem to trip off the tongue, or the page, far too easily. It is somewhat like the elevation of television presenters to stars, super-stars and even mega-stars, the higher the ascent, the stronger my doubt. There is one garden in particular which seems to have captured the market when it comes to descriptive praise. It is the "magnificent", "wild" and "magical" garden at Trebah, just a few miles to the south-west of Falmouth. At some time or another, over the last few years, Trebah has been called all of these things and more. The exciting thing is, every word is absolutely true. Whatever one says about Trebah, it simply is not enough to capture its full glory. The only way to do that is to visit and if you can manage to arrive on a day when bright sunshine reflects off the glossy hulls of yachts sailing down the Helford River, you will understand why Trebah is for many, the jewel in Cornwall's crown.

The origins of Trebah are lost in the mists of time. It is believed the name derives from the Cornish 'Tre Baya', meaning 'dwelling on the bay'. An apt description, the present house presides over a south facing, steep wooded ravine which drops almost two hundred feet to Polgwiddon Cove, a small sandy bay at the eastern end of the Helford Estuary. It was in the eighteenth century, when in the ownership of the Nicholl's family that the present landscape began to take shape. On virtually the only piece of level ground, at the head of the valley, the present white-painted, graceful, country house was built. In 1826, the house and wooded grounds were sold to a Quaker family from nearby Falmouth called Fox, and the rest, as they say, is history. The Foxes were an extraordinary family, creating a number of great gardens in the area, including Glendurgan, a garden now owned by the National Trust and situated just 500 yards east of Trebah. Charles Fox planted hundreds of *Pinus radiata*, Monterey Pine and *Pinus pinaster*, Maritime Pine, to act as shelter screens and then set about developing the area in the steep wooded ravine below the house, into a garden. It sounds quite simple. Today, those of us who develop a garden will sit down with a book, visit the local garden centre and possibly enlist the help of a landscape gardener to ensure the right plant goes into the right place. Charles Fox had other ideas, first he built, alongside the existing house, a large, red brick mansion, then from the top most windows, with the help of telescope and megaphone, he directed his army of gardeners in a military style planting operation across the twenty-five acre site. Many of the plants to go into the garden were seedlings, in some cases only inches tall, carefully collected from some mountainside or other in China, Japan or the Himalayan foothills by the great plant collectors of the day, including Joseph Hooker and Cornishman, William Lobb. What one has to bear in mind, is that these plants had never been grown in Britain before and so information on their growing requirements and eventual height and shape in maturity, was somewhat sketchy to say the least. Undaunted by all of this, Charles Fox had his gardeners scrambling and struggling up and down the steep slopes of the ravine, carrying wooden scaffolding towers, supposed to represent a particular plant in its maturity. Charles, carefully watching their progress through his telescope, would wait until the perfect spot was attained and then bark out his instructions over the megaphone. Bizarre to say the least, but it worked, many of the seedlings planted in this way are still there today, providing the backbone to Trebah's spectacular rhododendron flower displays.

When Charles Fox died in 1868, the estate passed to his son-in-law Edmund Backhouse, who continued to introduce new species to Trebah, including in 1890, three hundred *Dicksonia antarctica*, Soft tree ferns, from New South Wales. They were part of a consignment of three thousand which had been used as ballast on a ship travelling from Australia to England. The ship docked at Falmouth, where the ferns were off-loaded and shared out between ten of the best gardens in Cornwall. Today, more than one hundred years later, some of the batch planted at Trebah still survive, close on twenty feet tall with shaggy fibrous bark and fronds more than five feet long. They really are the most remarkable of plants, providing, from a distance, such an exotic statement to the landscape and then at close quarters revealing such delicate beauty, in the intricate web-like foliage of each individual frond. In 1906 the estate was sold to Charles Hext, a representative of one of Cornwall's oldest families. His first project was to dam the stream running down the centre of the ravine, creating a large pond just behind Polgwiddon Cove. Then, in a rather eccentric way, he attempted to bring more colour to the garden by stocking the pond with pink flamingos!

During the period 1900-1939 Trebah garden was really at the zenith of its first flowering incarnation. When villagers from the local hamlet of Mawnan Smith came to visit, they called it 'coming up paradise'. Plants were being introduced to Britain and consequently Trebah, at an

Previous pages 188. View from the top lawn down the valley to the Helford Estuary

incredible rate. Head Gardener Harry Thomas created many new cultivars, and planted the magnificent, deep pink flowered *Rhododendron* 'Trebah Gem', which towers over the ravine like some giant sentinel.

The outbreak of war in 1939 heralded the end to this golden period in Trebah's history. Gardening staff were called away to serve their country, few returning after the war. Inevitably the garden suffered, little maintenance occurred and a succession of owners virtually ignored the garden. In 1948, the red brick mansion, built by Charles Fox, burnt to the ground. The remains, along with the garden, began a gradual process of decay which was to last more than thirty years. Then in 1981, Trebah was purchased by Major Tony Hibbert MC and his wife Eira, as their retirement home.

It would be unfair to suggest, following on from Charles Fox and his megaphone and Charles Hext and his flamingos, that 1981 saw the arrival at Trebah of the third in a great line of eccentrics. However, the decision Tony Hibbert made shortly after his arrival, would have been considered, by some, the most eccentric act of all. Today, he delights in re-telling the story of how he and his wife purchased Trebah, as somewhere where they could forget about work, have no responsibilities or worries and just sit on the terrace of the original eighteenth century house. Ahead of them, so they thought, were blissful retirement days, drinking gin in the morning, wandering down through the jungle after lunch and then endless summer afternoons sailing their boat and fishing, and that was how it was, ... for a week. Then along came a chap from the Cornwall Garden Society to ask them how well plans were progressing for the restoration of one of the greatest gardens in Cornwall. Obviously seeing the disbelief and horror in their eyes, he gently lead the Hibberts down their own garden path, through the twenty-five acre 'jungle', showing them beneath thirty year old briars and brambles the defiant remains of a remarkable plant collection.

Back on the terrace, glass of gin in hand, the Hibberts realised they had two options. The first, to sell up as quickly as possible and get on with their retirement, or alternatively, sell the boat and forget about retirement for three years whilst they restored the garden. The chap from the Cornwall Garden Society suggested three years would just about see it through. In Tony Hibbert's own words, "of course we realised far too late, he was lying through his teeth", seventeen years later they are still at it. It took seven years just to clear the weeds and brambles to find out what was actually there. As they cleared, so apparently dead tree ferns sprung into life, rhododendron flowers appeared from nowhere and spring flowering daffodils and bluebells re-colonised the steep ravine sides. In 1987 they opened the garden to the public and by 1990 income raised from visitors ensured the garden could be self financing. So the Hibberts created a charity called 'The Trebah Garden Trust' in the same year and donated to it both the garden and the house. Thus making sure that the garden will be forever there for the enjoyment of others and, of course, no one will ever again have to give up their retirement in the way they had. When told in this way it sounds like a tremendous sacrifice and in many ways it was, however one only has to walk the gardens with Tony Hibbert to realise just how much he enjoyed the challenge. He has a great love and enthusiasm for his garden and is proud of his achievement, rightly so, because there really isn't anywhere quite like it in the world.

Just the walk from the car park to the entrance is enough to make one realise this is the beginning of something very special indeed. A narrow gravel path leads into a stone quarry area, which is smothered with plants rarely seen growing outdoors in Britain. Cordylines, echiums, agaves and aeoniums all provide a dazzling shop window display for both the garden and the plant centre alongside, where you purchase your ticket for the garden. At this point I bypass the cluster of wooden buildings comprising gift shop and café, they are for later, first of all the garden. I head along the Lawn Path which sweeps outwards around the flat lawn area immediately in front of the house. This is the very top of the ravine, some fifteen hundred yards below is the Helford River. In between the house and the river sits the most incredible garden vista imaginable. It is as if you have been transported half way across the world and are now staring down some remote Himalayan valley, although, when one starts to look closer, there are plants in this valley from all over the world. There are Himalayan rhododendrons, some of immense proportions over sixty feet tall, creating, in spring and early summer, a great cascading wave of colour which breaks upon the shore far below. Competing with the rhododendrons for the 'best flower at show' award, is a superb, *Acacia pravissima* from Australia, its golden yellow fragrant flowers radiant against the leathery evergreen foliage of a neighbouring, South American, eucryphia. The combination of so many exotic plants, in such a relatively small area, is breathtaking and if that were not enough then the sight of a group of Chusan Palms *Trachycarpus fortunei* from Central China, including at forty seven feet, the tallest in Britain, will knock you sideways.

It would be very easy to stop at this point and say, right that's it, I've seen it all, I've seen 'the enchanted garden'. What a great mistake that would be, for at every twist and turn in the grey gravelled path, new vistas and plant displays are revealed. I follow the Lawn Path up on round the house towards the Koi Pool. Here a sparkling spring tumbles out from between moss covered rocks into a deep pool overlooked by a bronze stork and containing thirty year old, salmon-pink and multi-coloured Koi Carp. This is a delightfully cool spot on a hot sunny day, with tree ferns and Japanese maples casting dappled shade upon those who sit mesmerised by the constant gliding passage of the carp. From here there is only one way to go and that is down, following the stream down into the very heart of the ravine. Along the way passing furcraeas, echiums and bright-eyed lampranthus, in a sub-tropical landscape reminiscent of Madeira. Paths lead off to the right and left but I'm heading for the Water Garden and Ninky's Pool. Ninky's Pool and further down, Dinky's Puddle are named after two Dutch girls, whose parents, members of the Dutch Resistance, helped Tony Hibbert when he escaped after being captured at Arnhem Bridge in 1944. In the Water Garden the stream edges are covered with masses of cream, trumpeted arum lilies, some three thousand in all, and even more candelabra primulas ranging in colour from the softest lemon to marmalade-orange. In spring, beneath a virtual plantation of tree ferns, great swathes of bluebells flank the path, to be followed within a month or two by golden drooping heads of *Crocosmia aurea*. Where the stream margins are at their boggiest, both the yellow spathed *Lysichiton americanus*, Skunk Cabbage and the white *Lysichiton camtschatcensis* proudly display side by side. From here on in one begins to understand why the word 'wild' so often appears in any half-decent description of Trebah. According to Tony Hibbert, if you can walk around a garden without getting your hair untidy and your clothes wet you are not in a proper garden. Well all I can say is by the time you stagger clear of The Bamboozle you will have seen a very proper garden indeed! At times, as you stoop low beneath thickets of bamboo, the path seems to disappear completely, but have courage, for once through, a spectacular horticultural delight awaits, a large *Davidia involucrata* Pocket Handkerchief Tree from China. If you happen to catch it in flower, when pure white drooping bracts dip low to mingle with bluebells around its base, then you too will know what it is like to be 'coming up paradise'.

In any other garden you would by now expect to have seen the best on offer, not so at Trebah, for it holds three of its finest features until the end. I have seen pretty big giant Brazilian Rhubarb, *Gunnera manicata* before, but never anything quite like this! If you dare, follow the path through the Gunnera Passage where the prickly stalks are as thick as your wrist and the leaves, sometimes eight feet across create a great green canopy high above one's head. It is like walking inside a giant green marquee, I'm certain if you took shelter here during the most torrential rain-storm, you would come out at the end as dry as a bone. Not that I would want to linger in the Gunnera Passage, there is something quite daunting being surrounded by this much vegetation. I know the guide book says they are kept well fed but ... well you never know!

Moving swiftly on, my triffid-like phobia is short-lived, for now one enters the Hydrangea Valley. Two acres of wall to wall mop-head hydrangeas encompassing Mallard Pond (they must have flown in when the flamingos left). This wonderful mix of Oxbridge blue and white flowers reflecting off the trout filled pond is not only stunning, it is also very clever. By planting literally hundreds of hydrangeas over the years, the Hibberts have extended the flowering season within the garden, from February and March when the *Campbellii* Magnolias begin to flower, right through to Christmas, when the colour finally fades from the hydrangeas. Where the hydrangeas end, the beach begins, and this really is the last of Trebah's surprises. For down here right on the banks of the Helford River, it feels much more like coast than river bank. A secluded sandy beach is accessible to visitors to the garden and is ideal for swimming and picnics.

In 1944 the 29th US Infantry Division left this beach bound for the D-Day assault on Omaha Beach in Normandy. As they looked back up the ravine towards the house on the day of their departure what view would they have seen? Probably a mature garden of unusual looking plants, with here and there the odd few bramble tendrils flexing their muscles. I wonder as they left, if any of them thought this might be a good place to retire to when it was all over?

After all ... they could drink gin on the terrace, sail and fish on the Helford River and simply watch the sun go down over the jungle ......

Opposite 189. View of the house from Petry's Path

190. The Chusan Palms *Trachycarpus fortunei*

191. Koi Pool with carp and Tree Ferns

192. Rhododendron Valley

193. Misty morning with *Rhododendron* 'Cornish Red'

194. *Magnolia stellata*

195. View to Helford Estuary past yellow *Acacia pravissima*

196. Bracts of the *Davidia involucrata*

197. *Gunnera manicata*

198. Gunnera Passage

199. Valley view with *Davidia involucrata* The Pocket Handkerchief Tree

200. Aquilegia and campion

201. Carpet of daffodils with a magnolia

202. Bluebells beneath a Beech tree overlooking the valley

204. The 'Fine Lace' of a Tree Fern

203. Tree Ferns below the Zig-Zag

205. Foxgloves with Tree Ferns

206. Arum Lilies in the Water Garden

207. Tree Ferns with *Crocosmia*

208. *Agapanthus* with Tree Ferns on the Zig-Zag

129

209. Arum Lily in the Water Garden

210. *Acacia pravissima*

211. Rhododendron flowers

212. Camellia

213. Tree Fern unfolding

214. Camellia

215. Late spring details with fallen petals

216. Arum Lilies with Candelabra Primulas and Foxgloves

217. Magnificent collection in Hydrangea Valley

131

Trengwainton

Trengwainton

It wasn't until fairly recently that I managed to visit Trengwainton for the first time. I had wanted to get there for years, but somehow it never seemed to happen. Whenever I came to Cornwall and worked my way down the peninsula, I would get as far as say, Trewithen or possibly Trebah and would then run out of time. It was always that bit further, in fact just about as far as one can go, being only seven miles or so from Land's End. Whenever I mentioned Trengwainton to anyone, the conversation normally went one of two ways. Either, 'never heard of it', or, I would see their eyes light up and we were off on a good hour's chat about the marvellous collection of tender plants in the walled gardens. Without doubt, Trengwainton is a plantsman's garden, it contains a vast array of sub-tropical plants, that in some cases, grow outside nowhere else on the British mainland. However, that does not mean it gets excluded from the list of gardens for those who simply want a nice day out. Quite the opposite in fact, it is a delightful garden, full of colour and interest, particularly, (and I would say this wouldn't I, as it's Cornwall), in the spring time which just happened to be the time of year when I finally managed to get there.

Trengwainton is a mile or so inland from Penzance, on ground rising to close on four hundred feet. Yes, it can be windy and it is, on the May afternoon I arrive. As I drive the Penzance to Morvan road, I can feel the car being pushed from side to side. Having seen the white, gatehouse entrance, I follow the signs to the car park, just a hundred yards or so up the road. Out of my car, jacket and waxproof on, I set off, down the narrow, high banked pathway towards the entrance. You can tell a lot about a garden, simply by looking at what they have for sale in their plant centre. The fact that some gardens do not have one, is not a problem. I would rather that was the case, than find just a clone of the garden centre down the road, with plants all bought in from one of the big wholesalers. Trengwainton has a small plant centre and it is good. Quite a lot of the stock looks 'home grown', and includes such choice plants as, *Acacia dealbata*, *Acacia melanoxylon*, *Myrtus lechleriana* and *Rhododendron fragrantissimum*.

Trengwainton is a long, linear garden. It sits either side of the tarmac road, which runs from the gatehouse to Trengwainton House. So the first thing, is to get off the road and plunge into the dense vegetation to the side. This I did and found myself in the Jubilee Garden, created to commemorate the Silver Jubilee of Queen Elizabeth II in 1977, (so the guide book says). Well you would never believe it, in here are Southern Beeches, *Nothofagus procera*, forty feet tall and an enormous Monterey Pine, *Pinus radiata*, that has to be one hundred years old, if it is a day. Perhaps the gravel tracks and the under plantings were put in in 1977. Whatever its age, there are some wonderful plants to see. Fine groups of *Phormiums*, the New Zealand Flax, with stiff, leathery sword-like leaves. Clusters of agapanthus, *crinums*, lilies and a superb *Pterostyrax hispida*, the Epaulette Tree, with drooping panicles of lovely, fragrant white flowers. The further I walk along this track the more exotic the scenery becomes. Bamboo, trained into archways, that I stoop to clear and as I emerge, a whole forest of *Dicksonia antarctica*, the Soft tree fern, beneath which runs a little rill, or stream, heading back towards the lodge gates. To the sides of the stream, the giant, rhubarb-like leaves, of *Gunnera manicata* and colourful drifts of astilbes cry out for your attention.

Gradually, the further west I travel, the more rhododendrons begin to appear, including a very old *Rhododendron rubiginosum*, propped up with stakes to prevent it sinking to the ground. Here too are *Rhododendron sinogrande* and one of my favourites, *Rhododendron macabeanum* with lovely pale-yellow, purple blotched flowers. Not only that, this plant is a layer from the original, introduced into Britain from Assam, by Frank Kingdon-Ward, in 1928. By a little wooden bridge crossing the stream, with tree ferns on either side, is a large *Podocarpus salignus*, a tender plant from Chile with lush, evergreen, willow-like foliage. Close by stands an interesting form of Lawson Cypress, the dreaded king of suburban hedges throughout the land. This variety is *Chamaecyparis lawsoniana* 'Intertexta' and has widely spaced, drooping branches that give it a graceful, weeping habit, but be warned, it grows almost as fast as the other one.

In places, where the topography allows, the little stream burbles and gurgles down tiny waterfalls, flights of stone steps and other little splashes. The path meanders back and forth, from the north to the south bank, over a succession of rustic bridges, until it finally breaks away from the woodland, to run through a close cut grassy meadow, running parallel to the main drive. This really is a delightful part of Trengwainton, all along the meandering water side, and quite often in it, are a whole host of water loving plants. Fleshy leaved hostas, cerise coloured astilbes, Royal Ferns, *Osmunda regalis* and hundreds upon hundreds of candelabra primulas, all coming together to produce a wonderful drift of colour which runs away into the distance. Where the

Previous pages 218. The Stream Garden with Candelabra Primulas meadow pushes the woodland back from the drive, so ornamental tree species creep in. A lovely golden Caucasian Maple, *Acer cappadocicum* 'Aureum' and just along the drive a superb *Acer palmatum* 'Atropurpureum', with such strident burgundy coloured foliage it seems almost to glow. A nice contrast is *Pinus patula*, the Mexican Weeping Pine, with beautiful, long fine needles and rich red bark. This particular specimen was planted by Her Royal Highness, The Princess Royal on 8th May 1972. As one approaches the house, so the wind starts to pick up. The smell of salt in the air is so powerful, it is almost overwhelming. Giant olearias, bedecked in white frothy flower, flail angrily in the gale and overhead ash branches, still not in leaf, clatter furiously.

There has been a house at Trengwainton since at least the sixteenth century. In 1814 the estate was bought by Rose Price, the son of a wealthy Jamaican sugar planter. He planted hundreds of trees around the estate, particularly ash, beech and sycamore for shelter and also built a series of walled gardens with raised sloping beds for growing early vegetables. In 1867 the property was bought by T S Bolitho, a banker with a family background in the Cornish tin mining industry. It was his son, Thomas Robins Bolitho, who built the present house, at the end of the last century. He also built the wide drive leading from the gatehouse to the main house. When Thomas Bolitho died in 1925, he left Trengwainton to his nephew, Lt-Col Sir Edward Bolitho. It was Sir Edward who transformed the garden, along with his Head Gardener, Alfred Creek. They obtained advice from J. C. Williams of Caerhays Castle and plants from Frank Kingdon-Ward's 1927-1928 expedition to north east Assam and the Mishmi Hills in Upper Burma. It is from seed, from this expedition, that many of the rhododendrons, now seen at Trengwainton were raised. The young plants being placed carefully within the sheltered plantations, created by Rose Price, more than one hundred years before. Quite a number of the plants raised from the 1927-28 expedition, flowered at Trengwainton, for the first time in the British Isles. Sir Edward used some of the walled gardens, again developed by Rose Price, to establish many of the more tender species. It was Sir Edward who opened up the stream which one follows virtually from the entrance. In 1965 he gave the house, the garden and the surrounding estate to the National Trust, ensuring that the garden would continue to be maintained and opened to the public. Sir Edward died in 1969 and his son Major Simon Bolitho, another knowledgeable plantsman and gardener, occupied Trengwainton until his death in 1991. His eldest son, Major Edward Bolitho now lives in the house, continuing the dedication and enthusiasm for the garden shown by his ancestors.

The house faces south, looking out over Newlyn and Penzance, across Mounts Bay to the Lizard Peninsula. In front of the house are lawns and to the side, terraces, with long sheltered borders. A rose pergola at the far end of the terraces is smothered with clematis, honeysuckle, jasmine and of course roses, all chosen to provide scent and colour over a long period of time. Behind the Higher Garden Lawn to the west of the house is a sheltered border containing the Magnolia Garden. Two wonderful specimens thriving in this area are the evergreen *Magnolia delavayi* and *Magnolia sargentiana* var. *robusta*, which has masses of large, deep pink flowers in April.

With the wind still increasing, (I can just imagine what it was like here during the gales of January 1990, when a large proportion of the original shelter trees were laid flat overnight), I decide retreat is the better part of valour. I set off down the Long Walk, a footpath heading eastwards from the lower lawn in front of the house. Within minutes I come across one of the most amazing trees I have ever seen. It is *Cryptomeria japonica* 'Elegans', surely the largest in the country, the trunk must be close on thirty inches diameter. The most wonderful thing about this tree is its bark, it is chestnut red and wavy beyond belief. It looks just like freshly combed auburn hair, running down a young girl's back.

The path dips and dives in every direction, passing an area where work is in progress to create an ornamental pond, adjacent to tree ferns and an exquisite specimen of *Rhododendron williamsianum*, with wonderful bronzy new foliage and delicate, pale pink, bell-shaped flowers. Where the foliage closes in on the path the fragrance from a bank of deciduous azaleas is intoxicating, even though many of the scented flowers have already fallen to the ground. As the rhododendron and azalea flowering season comes to an end, so the hydrangeas begin to flower, steel blue, purple, white and lime green varieties line the path sides, the sight must be quite magical in early summer when they are at their peak.

Crossing the drive, I make my way beneath the dark sombre bowers of the Camellia Walk. Of course in some parts of Britain camellias are still in flower, but down here, in the milder reaches of the south-west, the majority finished their spectacular displays weeks ago. Suddenly, beneath a large *Sophora japonica*, Japanese Pagoda Tree I notice an unusual looking tall shrub, with almost a Royal Fern-like leaf and a beautiful, small, lime-pink flower, it is like nothing I have seen before. A quick referral to my Hilliers manual confirms it to be *Lomatia ferruginea* a tender shrub from South America. From here on in I am constantly referring to my book, as I now enter one of the finest features at Trengwainton, the series of walled gardens to the north of the drive. They are exotic brick compartments with a climate all of their own and are indeed a plantsman's paradise. Within each brick walled compartment, are raised sloping beds, built by Rose Price for his early vegetables, more than one hundred and seventy five years ago. They are now treasure troves for some of the most exotic plants to be growing outside in mainland Britain. *Plagianthus regius*, from New Zealand, *Azara microphylla*, from Chile, *Melaleuca squarrosa*, from Australia, *Cestrum elegans* from Mexico, the list just keeps on growing and with it my sense of wonderment. Without doubt one of my favourite plants in this area is a small shrub, some eight feet tall, with delicate purple tinted white flowers and quite the most exquisite scent imaginable. It is *Prostanthera lasianthos* from Tasmania.

What a way to end my day at Trengwainton, an incredible experience. If they had floodlights I think I would be here all night. As I make my way back to my car, with dusk approaching, I ask myself just one question. Why did I ever leave it so long before visiting Trengwainton?

Opposite 219. *Acer palmatum* 'Atropurpureum' with azaleas and bluebells along The Drive

220. Stream Garden with Candelabra Primulas

221. Tree lined start to The Long Drive

222. Azaleas surrounded by bluebells

223. Stream Garden along The Drive

224. Azaleas by the Front Lawn

225. Walled garden with primroses and magnolia petals by a Dawn Redwood

226. Summer selection along the Stream Garden

227. Summer selection along the Stream Garden

228. Summer selection along the Stream Garden

229. Summer selection along the Stream Garden

230. Camellia

231. *Erythronium grandiflorum*

232. Camellia

233. Rhododendron beneath Tree Fern with bluebells

234. Close up of Azaleas

235. A small rhododendron

Tresco
Abbey

Tresco Abbey Gardens

Twenty six miles south west of Land's End, in the Atlantic Ocean, sits a cluster of small islands and islets, over 150 of them, collectively known as The Isles of Scilly. Only five are inhabited, St Martin's, St Agnes, Bryher, Tresco and the largest, St Mary's, which claims the only town, Hugh Town. The climate of these is islands is so mild, compared to the rest of Britain, that there is said to be only two seasons, spring and summer, temperatures seldom dipping below freezing. However, although frost may be virtually unheard of, the same cannot be said for wind. Severe, salt-laden gales frequently sweep over all the islands, keeping the vegetation low and in many instances, at a forty-five degree angle to the prevailing wind. All, that is, except Tresco, here on this tiny island, a mere two miles long and one mile wide, great windbreaks of *Cupressus macrocarpa*, Monterey Cypress, *Pinus radiata*, Monterey Pine and *Quercus ilex*, Holm Oak, have been planted, providing protection for one of the world's most incredible plant collections, the Tresco Abbey Gardens.

The simplest way to get to Tresco is to book a seat on the twenty-minute helicopter flight from Penzance. The helicopter lands literally at the garden gate. Alternatively, one can climb aboard the Scillonian 111, which sails from Penzance Harbour at 9.15am every morning from April to September. The crossing takes about two and a half hours, that is unless the wind decides otherwise. I had decided, long before my first visit to Tresco, that I wanted to arrive by sea. Yes, the helicopter is far more convenient but it didn't quite fit with the, 'Land Ahoy', romantic image I had of islands appearing on the blue horizon, nor the time-honoured approach through crystal clear waters full of dolphins and seals.

'Severe crossing, we advise passengers not to travel today' said a board as I walked down the Quay, and I was told that there was every likelihood the boat would not be able to dock when it eventually reached St Mary's. Somehow, up to three hours bobbing around the Atlantic, with a strong possibility of not even seeing Tresco at the end of it, did not appeal one bit. Reluctantly I made my way to the heliport, only to be told there were no available flights that morning. With my options narrowing rapidly, I contacted Land's End Aerodrome. Yes, flights were going to St Mary's, but whether anyone would be prepared to take me, by boat, across to Tresco was another matter. I decided to take the chance. An hour later, I found myself in a small Britten-Normander Islander, careering frantically down a grass runway towards the cliff edge. Far below, the sea was a white swirling cauldron, not a good omen but the touchdown on St Mary's was tame by comparison to the take-off from Land's End. Before too long we could see a small launch crashing through the waves towards us. A quick turn-around and we were on our last leg of the journey. As we chugged out of Hugh Town Harbour, someone asked which island was Tresco, the reply came swiftly back, "the one with trees on!" At one point we could see nothing at all, as an exceptionally large wave completely covered the launch, but we eventually came ashore at New Grimsby, the centre of population for Tresco's one hundred and thirty inhabitants. I set off along the coastline towards the Abbey Gardens, a mile or so away. Was it the fact that I was walking across almost pure white, fine grained sand, or was the weather beginning to brighten up? The wind did seem to have dropped somewhat and the sea now looked blue-grey instead of grey-white. It was still only 11am, there was hope yet for a decent day ahead.

White-washed cottages hugged the shoreline and in the soft dunes behind the beach, brilliant blue patches of early flowering agapanthus seemed to be growing everywhere, along with helichrysum, cordylines and yuccas. Suddenly from behind *Brachyglottis repanda*, the Pukapuka Bush from New Zealand, the turrets of the abbey gatehouse came into view. The abbey is the private residence of Robert Dorrien-Smith, the present lessee of Tresco and is not open to the public. Another New Zealand plant, *Griselinia littoralis* grows alongside colourful echiums, which seem to explode from between the giant bouldered abbey foundations and a charming group of *Olearia chathamica*, the Chatham Island Daisy Bush. In the space of five minutes I had seen three plants growing wild that were unlikely to survive a winter outside on the British mainland and I wasn't even inside the gardens!

Below the Eastern Rockery the track swings round to the right and heads for the garden entrance. On the wall is a slate tablet with the following inscription. "All islanders are welcome to walk in these grounds but are requested to keep to the main walks. Not to go up to the house nearer than the under terrace and to abstain from picking fruit or flowers, or scribbling nonsense and committing such like small nuisances. Enter then if it so please you and welcome". It did please me to enter and I made a mental note that, for today at least, I would refrain from scribbling nonsense.

Guide book in hand, I made my way directly to the ruins of St Nicholas Priory. Built in 1112 A.D. it is surprising to see so much of it

Previous pages 236. St. Nicholas Priory, the old Abbey ruins

still in existence, especially as the monks moved out as long ago as the late fifteenth century. The priory ruins now give protection and support for a whole world of plants and the walls are alive with just about every colour imaginable. Sky-blue flowers of *Ipomoea learii*, from tropical America, mix with the red, bottle-brush flowers of *Callistemon citrinus*, from Australia. Filling the smallest of cracks in the wall are delightful clumps of *Erigeron mucronatus*, the Mexican Daisy and alongside grows *Feijoa sellowiana*, the Pineapple Guava from Brazil, with its large dark red flowers bordered in white. *Arbutus unedo*, the Killarney Strawberry Tree is one of the few specimens I instantly recognise amongst this collection of sub-tropical plants. A word of advice; on your way to Tresco throw all your horticultural baggage overboard, because whatever knowledge of gardening you have, rest assured, it will be turned upside down on Tresco. Against a wide open sky that seems to be getting bluer by the minute, the graceful, feather-shaped arching leaves, up to fifteen feet long, of *Phoenix canariensis*, the Canary Island Date Palm, stands tall of the abbey ruins. Smaller, but none the less exotic is *Chamaerops humilis*, the Dwarf Fan Palm, from North America. Neither would stand much chance outside on the mainland, but on Tresco, where there are over three hundred growing days a year and even in the depths of winter the average temperature seldom dips below 5°c, they thrive. This was something discovered by Augustus Smith soon after he became Lord Proprietor of all the Isles of Scilly in 1834. He chose to live on Tresco, building his house on a rocky outcrop directly above the ruins of St Nicholas Priory and calling it Tresco Abbey. Once the house was built, he turned his attention to the garden, initially creating a series of walled enclosures around the priory ruins. Then he built three long terraces on the adjacent, tree-less, south-facing slope, linking each terrace together with flights of stone steps. Finally, he began planting windbreaks on the western boundary, to help lift the prevailing wind up and right over the garden.

By 1855 the garden had grown to its present seventeen acres and already contained thriving collections of exotic plants from as far away as North Africa, the Canary Islands and South America, including the magnificent *Puya alpestris* from Chile. Today, this evergreen perennial, with its great spikes of stunning jade-green waxy flowers, still brings gasps of admiration from those lucky enough to catch it in flower in early summer. Can you imagine the excitement at Tresco one hundred and forty years ago when it flowered for the very first time in Britain. By 1872, the year Augustus died, the exotic nature of the garden was widely known and already attracting visitors. Five generations later, the present family member responsible for Tresco is Robert Dorrien-Smith, who has to look after 30,000 visitors a year. His Head Gardener, now Curator, is Mike Nelhams, who has total responsibility for maintaining this unique collection of twenty thousand exotic plants. Occasionally, Mike and his team of five gardeners have to deal with catastrophes, as in January 1987 when between seventy and eighty per cent of the exotic plants in the garden were lost as temperatures plummeted to -8°c. Three years later the gales which hit southern Britain, blew down virtually half of the original shelter trees. It is to Mike Nelham's credit that on this late June day, as I make my way from the old abbey ruins down towards the Hop Circle, I can see little sign of either natural disaster.

Passing through the Long Walk, which is the main axis of the garden and marks the boundary for the lower of the three terraces, the view is without doubt one of the most improbable landscapes one is likely to witness in a British garden. It looks just about as tropical as you can get, indeed it has been described in the past as 'the Temperate House at Kew Gardens without the glass', and one can understand why, there are just so many palms, succulents and other curious looking plants along its length. Within seconds I am hurrying to identify a small tree with wonderful delicate foliage, it is *Acacia filicifolia*, the Fern-Leaved Wattle. Alongside is *Pseudopanyx crassifolium*, a New Zealand tree almost thirty feet tall with superb slender, evergreen leaves, which cast dappled shade onto the glorious bright orange flowers of *Jovellana violacea* from Chile. Another plant, with unusual rhododendron-like leaves and peach-coloured foxglove-like flowers, grows close by, it is *Isoplexus canariensis*, as one would expect, originally from the Canary Islands. I pass under an enormous *Banksia integrefolia* from Australia, with lime-yellow bottle-brush flowers high above my head, this specimen is believed to be the largest in existence, and by sheer chance I end up in the Hop Circle. The hops have long gone, replaced by a hedge of bay, *Laurus noblis*. Inside grows a ring of some twenty mature Chusan Palms, *Trachycarpus fortunei* interspersed with *Chamaerops humilis*. In the centre of the circle are two wonderful specimens of the purple-leaved, New Zealand Cabbage Palm, *Cordyline australis* 'Purpurea'. Seeing really is believing, it is astonishing to find plants like this growing to such a size in the open, only twenty-six miles from the British mainland.

Returning to the Long Walk, I can see blue sky through the palm leaves overhead, and the occasional shaft of sunlight filters through the foliage to the white gravelled path below. It is difficult to know where to go to next, there are just so many wondrous things to see in every direction. Instinctively, I start to head towards the higher terraces and the views so often photographed, across the garden to the sea. Turning onto the Lighthouse Path, right in the heart of the garden, I meet with Mike Nelhams. His enthusiasm is infectious, almost at a gallop he guides me round his garden, throwing out botanical names and exotic sounding places as if his life depended on it. He is a man of many parts. He controls the helicopter movements in and out of Tresco, mans the fire tender when necessary, can be found leading a guided tour of the Mediterranean, or perhaps in London judging for the Royal Horticultural Society. I asked him which is his favourite month at Tresco, and we ended up working through the whole calendar. In truth, he loves Tresco dearly at any time of year. There are different plants in flower here all year round. A few years ago a survey of those plants in flower on New Year's Day was carried out. The total was in excess of three hundred, which is comparable with La Mortola on the Italian Riviera. Tresco can actually grow a far greater range of plants to those found in Mediterranean regions. The lower garden provides ideal humid conditions for plants from New Zealand and South America, whilst the upper terraces, which tend to be hot and dry, suits South African and Australian plants. Not only that, a lot of the material grown at Tresco is endangered in the wild, for example *Geranium maderense*, which is extremely rare in its native land of Madeira but at Tresco it grows like a weed.

As I approach 'Father Neptune', the wooden figurehead from the S.S. Thames, wrecked on the Western Rocks of Scilly in 1841, and now guarding the approach to the Top Terrace, I am overwhelmed by the sheer beauty of Tresco. In every direction there are plant displays like no other. Giant, granite rockeries are brimming with echiums, fucraeas, agapanthus, aeoniums and *Strelitzia reginae*, the Bird of Paradise flower from South Africa. It seems no country is out of bounds for Tresco, *Saurauja subspinosa*, with its rough leathery rhododendron-like leaves from Upper Burma, *Euphorbia annal*, a succulent cactus-like plant from Saudi Arabia and *Brahea armata*, the magnificent big blue Hespa Palm from Mexico all flourish here. Perhaps the most stunning plants of all are the New Zealand Flame Trees, *Metrosideros robusta*. With pillar-box red, bottle-brush fragrant flowers, they look absolutely fantastic against the clear, deep blue Tresco sky. Before the frosts of 1987 some were over eighty feet tall, many succumbed to that cold winter, others were severely cut back. Ten years on, the re-growth is incredible, some are already forty feet tall and are flowering like mad.

From the top terrace, the views out across the palms to the azure sea and the white, sand-fringed islands of Bryher, Samson and beyond to St Mary's are breathtaking. It is hard to believe the weather conditions I arrived in only six hours ago. Then, was the nearest thing Tresco experiences to winter; now, it is the gentle end to a glorious summer's day, a day that has been like no other. I make my way slowly down through the recently created Mediterranean Garden. Here, a terracotta roofed summerhouse sits on a white gravel terrace edged with a stone balustrade. On the terrace below, young olive trees and Pencil Cypress, *Cupressus sempervirens*, have been planted. Large terracotta pots flank stone steps leading down to a pool, the central feature of which is a splendid bronze fountain in the shape of an agave plant. The effect is quite amazing, had I not known, I would have said the Mediterranean Garden has always been here, it sits so effortlessly within its surroundings.

There are more Pencil Cypress trees in an intimate little garden close to the Lighthouse Walk, this time combining with great swathes of lavender. Nearby there is a delightful stone sculpture of a woman sitting, called 'Gaia'. The grain of the rock she has been hewn from, running from her outstretched arm, across her face and rippling across her breasts. Soon, I reach the southern boundary of the garden at Valhalla, an open-sided building which houses a collection of ships figureheads, from wrecks on the Scilly coastline over the last three hundred years. Each one has been lovingly restored, responsibility for the collection now resting with the National Maritime Museum. From here, the start of my journey home is just yards away. Alongside the exit from the garden sits another quite wonderful sculpture, this time in bronze, created by David Wynne in 1990. It portrays the three children of Robert Dorrien-Smith, enjoying the freedom of this magical island.

On the launch heading from Tresco back to St Mary's, I strain my eyes to catch just one last glimpse of colour between the pines and evergreen oaks of the shelter belt. I am only five minutes into my journey and already missing Tresco.

I wonder how soon I can return?

Opposite 237. The Middle Terrace showing a selection of what is so unique and special to the Abbey Gardens

239. *Metrosideros robusta*

238. *Chasmanthe bicolor* with *Echiums pininiana*

240. Pergola on the Middle Terrace

241. Flame Trees with St. Mary's on the horizon

242. *Butia capitat*a in the Pebble Garden

243. Middle Terrace with *Agave*, *Gazania* and South African *Pelargonium*

149

244. *Phoenix canariensis, Cordyline australis* and *Agapanthus*

245. *Hydrangea* and *Codyline* in the Lily Garden

246. Summer House on the Middle Terrace

247. South African pink *Pelargonium*

248. Neptune Steps

151

249. *Yucca* with *Pelargonium*

250. *Agapanthus* and *Furcraea* on West Rockery

251. Canary Island *Aeonium*

252. *Watsonia* 'Tresco Hybrid' with St. Mary's in the background

253. Agave bronze fountain in the Mediterranean Garden

254. Upper Terrace of the Mediterranean Garden

255. Upper Terrace of the Mediterranean Garden

256. Looking down on the terraced Mediterranean Garden

153

258. *Butia capitata* in the Pebble Garden

257. *Echium pininiana*

154

259. *Gazania*

260. *Aeonium*

261. *Gazania*

262. *Callistemon citrinus*

263. *Gazania splendeni*

264. *Pelargonium capitatum*

PHOTOGRAPHER'S NOTES

For me, photography is about light, colour, the right moment and magic.

Sometimes when the right light, colours and opportunity come together in a special place, you really can find magic. It can be at any time, in any weather and surprisingly when least expected. It will appear, sometimes for a few minutes, sometimes longer – you must be ready, know your camera and equipment, and to work quickly and intuitively. When that magic does appear, it is like some very special gift, presented on a beautiful stage – it is Nature. To quote Minor White "Each artist going in his own direction at some time Walks on water'.

My visits to Cornwall have given me many moments of that special magic, I have found it a wonderful experience to have the privilege of visiting the gardens, often early in the morning or late in the evening when I am the only visitor. From so many special and unique gardens it has been very difficult to decide on which to include or exclude but in the end it has been a personal decision. I am sure that many people will have an opinion and comment on the gardens that have been included and the gardens that have been left out. My approach is inspirational and rather than do little justice to many I prefer to limit the selection and to be able to get to know a garden intimately and show it through the seasons in its various moods and conditions. I like to walk the garden and 'sketch' with my 35mm camera returning later with the appropriate larger format camera when the light and conditions are right. After all the time and effort it takes to create a garden the least I can do is to respect this and take the time to record it properly.

For the gardener and garden photographer Cornwall is quite special. Nowhere is there such a concentration of wonderful and diverse gardens and conditions to see and to photograph, from Lanhydrock, close to Bodmin Moor in the east, with its lush greens and climate influenced by the mists and higher rainfall to the quite unique Abbey Garden on Tresco in the west. The rewards for the little effort and expense of visiting Tresco in the beautiful Isles of Scilly, swept by the Gulf Stream, are more than you can imagine and well worthwhile.

For practical photographic help I must say, for me, my best pictures are taken when I am at one with the garden or landscape being able to really feel and see Nature. Shutter speeds and "F" numbers are, at such times, not part of my conscious record – they are information from the light meter which is transferred to the camera at that moment and is special and relevant only to that moment of time. Again to quote the great American photographer Minor White in his book "Rites & Passages" (published by Aperture of N.Y.), "For technical data – the camera was faithfully used".

I use, mostly for reference and "sketching", a 35mm Nikon camera. For the pictures in this book I have used the larger formats of the Hasselblad 6 x 6cm with the Fuji 6 x 9cm 90mm and Fuji 6 x 17cm 105mm cameras. The film used has been Fuji Provia. My most important photographic equipment is a strong tripod, giving me time to compose and consider, a polarizer filter to cut out most of the unwanted reflections and improve colour (the cheapest and most effective way to improve garden and landscape photography) and a cable release. The only other, though most important ingredient is time and patience.

If the pictures in this book inspire you and you get half the pleasure and satisfaction that I have had from visiting and photographing these great and wonderful gardens of Cornwall I am sure that the foresight and vision of the original creators will last and be appreciated by future generations.

Derek Harris. January 1998.

ACKNOWLEDGEMENTS

We would like to thank The National Trust and the owners of the gardens presented in this book for the opportunity and privilege of visiting and recording their gardens. To acknowledge the debt and gratitude we must all have to them and their predecessors who have created and maintained, through much hard work, patience and investment these very special and unique Cornish gardens.

We would also like to thank and acknowledge all the gardeners whose painstaking efforts, through all weathers and conditions, make these great gardens a pleasure to visit. Without them these gardens would soon be "lost".

To His Royal Highness, The Prince of Wales for his splendid Foreword.

Our special thanks for the help, advice and encouragement in the preparation of this book must go to Tony and Eira Hibbert, Philip Tregunna, Mike Nelhams, Giles Clotworthy and Phillip Hunt.

Derek Harris and Tony Russell. January 1998.

My love and personal thanks to Rosemary for all her help, encouragement and tremendous support, not only during the preparation of this book but throughout the last few somewhat hectic years!

To Lyn McCracken for her dedication and patience during the preparation of the typescript and for her wonderful enthusiasm and ability to always be there in a crisis!

Finally, to my grandfather for his influence and of course his garden.

Tony Russell.

My personal thanks to Esther Marshall for her help and encouragement when the photography turned to sorting and checking!

To Chris Richardson, Andy Jolley, Del Mason and all at Goodfellow & Egan in Peterborough who worked on the Origination and Typesetting for their personal interest in the preparation of this book.

Finally to thank Eric Carr and his worthy assistant for the continued first class service and E6 processing at 42 Bluebell Avenue, Peterborough, PE1 3XQ.

Derek Harris. January 1998.

GLOSSARY OF BOTANICAL NAMES

Abutilon x suntense 'Jermyns' 99
Acacia dealbata 134
Acacia filicifolia 145
Acacia meladroxylon 134
Acacia pravissima 19,31,121,**125**, **130**
Acer campestre 31,41
Acer cappadocicum 'Aureum' 135
Acer forestii 42
Acer griseum 18,32,42
Acer japonicum 99
Acer japonicum 'Aconitifolium' 41
Acer maximowiczianum 67
Acer palmatum 20,87,99
Acer palmatum 'Atropurpureum' 135,**92,137**
Acer palmatum 'Dissectum' 30
Acer palmatum 'Sango Kaku' 41,**48**
Acer rubescens 76
Actinidia chinensis 42
Aeonium **152,155**
Aesculus indica 78
Agapanthus 19,**104,129**, **150,152**
Agave americana **61**,111
Ailanthus altissima 99,111
Alstroemeria **104**
Anemones 18
Aralia elata 'Variegata' 20
Araucaria araucana 100
Arbutus unedo 145
Arbutus x andrachnoides 19
Astilbes **107,114**
Aubretia 20
Azara integrifolia 98
Azara lanceocata 78
Azara microphilla 136
Azara serrata 99,100,**107**
Banksia integrefolia 145
Berberis thunbergii 'Rose Glow' 78
Betula 78
Betula ermanii 32
Betula maximowicziana 78
Betula utilis 20,32
Brachyglottis repanda 144
Brahea armata 146
Butia capitata **149,154**
Callistemon bigiou 31
Callistemon citrinus 145,**155**
Cambellii 32
Camellia 'Anticipation' 32
Camellia 'Brigadoon' 68
Camellia 'Captain Rawes' 110
Camellia 'Cornish Snow' 19, 110
Camellia 'Debbie' **83**
Camellia 'Debutante' 110
Camellia 'Donation' 78
Camellia 'Dream Castle' 68,**73**
Camellia 'Elizabeth Johnstone' 78

Camellia 'Glenn's Orbit' **50**,78
Camellia 'Joan Trehane' **83**
Camellia 'Trewithen Pink' 78
Camellia 'Ville de Nantes' 110
Camellia japonica **50**,66,68
Camellia japonica 'Alba Simplex' 68
Camellia japonica 'Lady Clare' **50**
Camellia japonica 'Margaret Rose' 32
Camellia japonica 'Pink Perfection' 110
Camellia reticulata 'Butterfly Wings' 110
Camellia reticulata 'Captain Rawes' 42
Camellia reticulata 'Crimson Rose' 110
Camellia reticulata 'Lavinia Massi' 110
Camellia reticulataa 'Lion's Head' 110
Camellia saluenensis 66,68
Camellia x williamsii 66,68
Camellia x williamsii 'Brigadoon' 32
Canna **106**
Cardiocrinum giganteum 42
Cautleya spicata 99,**107**
Ceanothus arboreus 'Trewithen Blue' 77,**83**
Cedrus atlantica 'Glauca' 32
Cedrus deodara 112,**114**
Ceonothus 18,**41**
Cercidiphyllum japonicum 'Pendulum' 112
Cercidiphyllum japonicum 20,31
Cercis siliquastrum 111
Cestrum aurantiacum 98
Cestrum elegans 136
Chamaecyparis lawsoniana 'Intertexta' 135
Chamaecyparis pisifera 'Filifera' 99
Chamaerops humilis 145
Chasmanthe bicolor **148**
Choisya ternata 19
Clematis armandii 77
Clematis rehderiana 98
Clianthus puniceus 18,77,**83**
Colchicum 19
Cordyline australia 'Purpurea' 145,**150**
Cornus capitata 'Bentham's Cornet' 54
Cornus controversa 'Variegata' 76
Cornus kousa 41,42,111
Corylopsis glabrescens 41
Corylopsis willmottiae 20
Craetagusmonosyna 'Biflora' 111
Crinodendron hookerianum 19
Crocosmia aurea **129**
Cryptomeria japonica 98
Cryptomeria japonica 'elegans' 136
Cunninghamia lanceolata 112
Cupressus macrocarpa 99,**104**,144
Cupressus sempervirens 146
Cyathea australis 112
Cyathodes colensoi 112
Cyclamen 19
Cytisus 'Porlock' 99
Cytisus battandieri 31
Dacridium franklinii 87
Davidia involucrata 20,56,76,

Davidia involucrata 122,**126**
Deutzia x hydrida 'Perle Rose' 42
Dicksonia antarctica 20,**62,63**,67, 78,100
Drimys lanceolata 19,87
Drimys winteri 'Winters Bark' 99
Echiums pininiana **148,154**
Embothrium coccinetum 78,111
Enkianthus campanulatus 41,78
Enkianthus cernuus var. 'rubens' 20
Enkianthus deflexus 87
Erica Arborea var. 'alpina' 20
Erigeron mucronatus 145
Erythronium grandiflorum **141**
Eucryphias 31
Euphorbia annal 146
Feijoa sellowiana 145
Fraxinus excelsior 'Jaspidea' 19
Fremontedendron californicum 31
Fuchsias 19
Furcraea 142
Gazania **149,155**
Geranium maderense 146
Ginkgo biloba 31,32,87
Gleditsia japonica 19
Griselinia littoralis 19,144
Gunnera manicata 20,56,100, 122,**126**
Gypsofila **104**
Hakea lissosperma intro
Halesia carolina 100
Hemerocallis 31
Hoherias 31
Holboellia latifolia 31
Hostas 20
Hydrangea 20,**61,103,106**, **107,131,150**
Hydrangea aspera 42
Hydrangea paniculata 81
Hydrangea petiolaris 18
Ipomoea learii 145
Isoplexus canariensis 145
Jovellana violacea 145
Juglans nigra 30,31
Kniphofias 19
Koelreuteria paniculata 19,31
Laurus noblis 145
Leptospermum scoparium 25
Liatris spicata 'Gay feathers' 99,**103,106**
Liquidambar styraciflua 77
Liriodendron tulipifera 19,112
Lithocarpus pachyphyllus 67
Lomatia ferruginea 87,136
Lysichiton americanus 20,**62**,78,**83**, 87,**90,92**,122
Lysichiton camtschatcensis 87,**95**,122
Magnolia veitchii 67
Magnolia ashei 41
Magnolia campbellii **49**,55,67,68,87

Magnolia campbellii var. mollicomata 78
Magnolia campbellii
  'Caerhays Surprise' 68,**72**
Magnolia dawsoniana 41
Magnolia delavayi 41,136
Magnolia denudata 31
Magnolia grandiflora 30,31
Magnolia grandiflora 'Gallissonière' 99
Magnolia hypoleuca 42,87
Magnolia liliflora 32
Magnolia liliflora 'Nigra' 41
Magnolia macrophylia dealbata 87
Magnolia sargentiana 67
Magnolia sargentiana var. robusta 136
Magnolia x soulangeana 20,87
Magnolia x soulangeana 'Lennei' 42
Magnolia x soulangeana
  'Rustica Rubra' 42
Magnolia sprengeri 'Diva' 78
Magnolia sprengeri 67
Magnolia stellata **95,125**
Magnolia wilsonii 78,87
Magnolia x veitchii 32,41,68
Melaleuca squarrosa 136
Metasequoia glybtostroboides 20,32,42
Metrosideros robusta 146,148
Michelia doltsopa 32,68,**69,80**
Michelia doltsopa flowers **73,80**
Morus nigra 31
Musa basjoo 112
Myrtus lechleriana 32,76,134
Myrtus luma 76,87,99
Narcissi 18,19,66,99
Nacissi 'Irene Copeland' 100
Narcisi 'Mary Copeland' 100
Nepeta sintenisii 'Six Hills Giant' 30
Nothofagus 78
Nothofagus dombeyi 32
Nothofagus menziesii 78
Nothofagus nervosa 78
Nothofagus procera 134
Olearia chathamica 144
Osmanthus burkwoodii 41
Osmanthgus delavayi 42
Osmunda regalis 41,135
Paliurus-spina-christi 111
Papavers 19
Parottia persica 41
Paulownia tomentosa 42,78,112
Pelargonium **149,151,152**, **155**
Philadelphus 31,41
Phoenix canariensis 145,**150**
Phormiums 134
Photina x fraseri 'Red Robin' 100
Picea breweriana 42
Pieris formosa var. forrestii 76,77
Pieris 'Forest Flame' **70**
Pinus bhutanica 87

Scientific name	Page(s)
Pinus patula	20,135
Pinus pinaster	120
Pinus radiata	19,40,78,111
Piptanthus nepalensis	78
Plagianthus regius	136
Platanus orientalis	31
Podocarpus salignus	18,135
Podocarpus totara	56
Polygonatum x hybridum	100
Polystichum setiferum	20
Poncirus trifoliata	31
Primula	20,68,**73**
Primula candelabra	**47,131,132,133,138,140**
Primula 'Garryarde Guineven'	99
Prostanthera lasianthos	136
Prunus 'Kanzan'	99,**105**
Prunus 'Tai Haku'	99,**105**,112,**115**
Prunus incisa	112
Prunus serrula	42
Pseudopanyx crassifolium	145
Pterostxray hispida	134
Puya alpestris	145
Pyrus nivalis	31
Quercus cerris	100
Quercus ilex	30,100,111,121
Quercus suber	19,31
Rehderodendron macrocarpum	78
Rhododendron 'Cornish Red'	23,55,**57,62,81,86,91**,99,112,**125**
Rhododendron 'Crossbill'	66
Rhododendron 'Goldsworth Yellow'	**83**
Rhododendron 'Gwilt King'	100
Rhododendron 'Mary Swaythling'	100
Rhododendron 'Polar Bear'	112
Rhododendron 'Trebah Gem'	121
Rhododendron arboreum	32,86,99
Rhododendron augustinii	100
Rhododendron catawbiense	86
Rhododendron fragrantissimum	134
Rhododendron griffithianum	32
Rhododendron johnstoneanum	100
Rhododendron kewensi	32
Rhododendron lutescens	66,68
Rhododendron macabeanum	32,134
Rhododendron pachytrichum	87,**92,95**
Rhododendron ponticum	40
Rhododendron quinquefolium	87
Rhododendron rubiginosum	134
Rhododendron russellianum	**27**
Rhododendron schippenbachii	32
Rhododendron sinogrande	55
Rhododendron sino-grande	134
Rhododendron spinuliferum	66
Rhododendron thomsonii	100
Rhododendron williamsianum	32,136
Robina hispida	20
Rosa chinensis 'Mutabilis'	98
Saurauja subspinosa	146
Sedum spectabile 'Autumn Joy'	42
Sophora tetraptera	31
Sorbus discolor 'Joseph Rock'	42
Sprengeri	32
Stachys byzantina	20
Styrax japonica	87,**93**
Strelitzia reginae	146
Stuartia sinensis	78
Suphora japonica	136
Taxodium distichum	42,112,**115**
Taxus baccata var. fastigiata	41
Taxus baccata 'Dovastroniana'	32
Thuja plicata	111
Tillia x euchlora	30
Trachycarpus fortunei	19,55,**62**,100,111,**124**
Tsuga canadensis	32
Viburnum plicatum 'Mariesii'	87,**91**,111,**117**
Viburnum x burkwoodii	99
Viburnum betulifolium	78
Watsonia 'Tresco Hybrid'	
Wisteria sinensis	68,77,**90**
Yucca	**152**

COMMON NAMES

Common name	Page(s)
Australian Tree Fern	112
Arum Lilies	129,130,131
Azaleas	40,42,68,77,100
Bamboo	56,100,112,122,134
Banana Bush	112
Begonias	44
Bhutan Pine	86
Bird of Paradise flower	146
Black Walnut	30,31
Bluebells	**22,47,108/109**
Blue Cedar	32
Brazilian Rhubarb	122
Brewers Spruce	42
'Brown Turkey' fig	99
Cabbage Palm	145
Californian lilac	77
Camellias	32,40,42,66,68,77,110,136
Canary Island Date Palm	145
Causican maple	135
Catmint	**37**
Century Plant	111
Chatham Island Daisy Bush	144
Cherry Blossom	**96/97,105,117**
Cherry Laurel	111,116
Chile Pine	100
Chilean Fire Bush	78,111
Chilean Lantern Bush	19
Chinese Dogwood	41,42
Chinese Firs	112
Chinese Gooseberry	42
Christ's Thorn	111
Chusan Palm	19,55,100,111,121,145
Clematis	**24**
Copper Beaches	41
Cork Oak	31
Cypress Trees	**10/11**
Daffodils	**16/17,127**
Dawn Redwood	20,42
Dwarf Fan Palm	145
Eastern Hemlock	32
Epaulette Tree	134
Fern-Leaved Wattle	145
Field Maple	31,41
Foxglove Tree	42,78,112
Glastonbury Thorn	111
Golden Ash	19
Great White Cherry	112
Hespa Palm	146
Himalayan birch	20,32
Himalaya Tanbark Oak	67
Holm Oak	30,32,100,111,144
Huon Pine	87
Indian Cedar	112
Indian Horse Chestnut	78
Irish Yews	41
Japanese acers	78
Japanese Angelica trees	20,**27**
Japanese Bitter Orange	31
Japanese Cedar	98
Japanese Cherry	42,99
Japanese Dogwood	111
Japanese Locust trees	19
Japanese Maple	20,30,87,99,122
Japanese Pagoda Tree	136
Japanese Rowan	42
Judas Tree	111
Katsura Tree	20,31,112
Killarney Strawberry Tree	145
Lavender	**10/11**
Lawson Cypress	135
Lily Tree	31
Lobster Claw	18,77
Magnolia	18,20,31,40,41,42,66,67,68,78,122
Maidenhair Tree	31,33
Maritime Pine	120
Mediterranean Cork Oaks	19
Mexican Daisy	145
Mexican Orange Blossom	19
Mexican Weeping Pine	135
Mock Orange	31,41
Monarch birch	78
Monterey Cypress	144
Monterey Pine	18,40,78,111,120,134,144
Mount Fuji Cherry	112
Mulberry	31
Myrtle	54,76,87
New Zealand Flame Tree	146
New Zealand Flax	134
New Zealand Totara Tree	56
Nikko Maple	67
Orchids	**1**,94,116,117
Oriental Plane	31
Oven's Wattle	19
Paperback Maple	18,32,42
Pencil Cypress	146
Persian Ironwood	41
Pineapple Broom	31
Pineapple Guava	145
Pocket Handkerchief Tree	20,56,76,122
Podocarpus	18
Pride of India	19,31
Primroses	**71,116**
Pukapuka Bush	144
Rhododendron	18,20,40,42,54,55,66,67,68,77,86,98,99,100,111,112,120
Rose Acacia	20
Rose Albertine	41,**44**
Rose Floribunda	**27**
Royal Fern	41,135
Russian Rock Birch	32
Silver beech	78
Skunk cabbage	20,**83**,87,**90,92**,122
Snake Bark Maple	42
Snowdrop Tree	100
Soft Tree Fern	20,100,112,120,134
Solomon's Seal	100
Southern beech	134
Spread-Leaved Pine	20
Strawberry Tree	19
Swamp Cypress	42,112
Sweet William	**60,61**
Tradescantia	**106**
Tree of Heaven	111
Tibetan Cherry	42
Tree Ferns	**8**,56,67,122,**128,130**
Tree Heathers	20
Tree Of Heaven	99
Tree Rhododendrons	20,32,54,78,99
Tulip 'China Pink'	**51**
Tulip 'West Point'	**51**
Tulip Tree	19,112
Turkey Oaks	100
Verbena	**106**
Weeping lime	30
Western Red Cedar	111
Westfelton Yew	32

PEOPLE

Backhouse, Edmund	120	Earl of Mount Edgcumbe	20	James Veitch and Sons	66,68	Repton, Humphrey	30
Bolitho, Lt-Col Sir Edward	135	Edgcumbe, Sir Richard	20	Johnstone, George	78,87	Smit, Tim	54,55,56
Bolitho, Major Edward	135	Edgcumbe family	18	Kindon-Ward, Frank	87,134,135	Smith, Augustus	145
Bolitho, Major Simon	135	Forrest, George	66,68,110	Lawrence, Captain John	98	Thomas, Harry	121
Bolitho, T.S.	135	Fox, Alfred	110,111,112	Lilly, Jack	100	Thomas, John	86
Bolitho, Thomas Robins	135	Fox, Charles	120,121,111	Lobb, William	120	Thomas, Simon	31
Borlase, Peter	42	Fox, George	110,111	Lord Rosebery	41	Thomas-Peter, John	86
Carew-Pole Garden Trust	30,31	Fox, Sarah	111	Nash, John	66	Trebah, Garden Trust, The	121
Carew-Pole, Lady	31	Galsworthy, A.M.J.	76,78	National Maritime Museum	146	Tregunna, Philip	66,67,68
Carew-Pole, Lady Cynthia	31	Gilbert, Carew Davies	98,100	National Trust	18,30,40,41,98,	Trevanion, John Bettesworth	66
Carew-Pole, Sir John	30	Gilbert, John Davies	98		110,111,112,135	Williams, Charles	66
Carew-Pole, Sir Richard	30	Gladstone, William	41	Nelhams, Mike	145,146	Williams, J.C.	66,68,87,135
Copeland, Ida	98	Hext, Charles	120,121	Nelson, John	54,55,56	Williams, John Michael	66
Copeland, Ronald	98	Hibbert, Eira	121	Parsons, Jaimie	66	Williams, Julian, C.B.E.	66,67
Creek, Alfred	135	Hibbert, Major Tony, MC	121	Pole-Carew, General Sir Richard	31	Williams, Michael	66
Cunliffe, Leonard Daneham	98	Hillier, Harold	87	Pole-Carew, Rt. Hon Reginald	30	Wilson, E.H.	66,68
Daniell, Ralph Allen	98	Holman, Nigel	86,87	Pole-Carew, Sir William	30	Wynne, David	146
Dorrien-Smith, Robert	145,146	Holman, Treve	86	Price, Rose	135		
Earl of Falmouth	98	Hooker, Joseph	120	Pye, William	30		
		HRH The Princess Royal	76,135	Queen Elizabeth II	134		

265. Churchyard at Lanhydrock

"Let children walk with Nature, let them see the beautiful blendings and communions of death and life, their joyous inseparable unity, as taught in woods and meadows, plains and mountains and streams of our blessed star, and they will learn that death is stingless indeed, and as beautiful as life............All is divine harmony".   John Muir.